It Gives Me Great Pleasure

The complete after-dinner speaker's handbook

HERBERT PROCHNOW

PIATKUS

First published in Great Britain by
Judy Piatkus (Publishers) Ltd of
5 Windmill Street, London W1

First paperback edition 1994

**The moral right of the author
has been asserted**

*A catalogue record for this book
is available from the British Library*

ISBN 0-7499-1079-8 hbk
ISBN 0-7499-1392-4 pbk

Set in 12/13 Compugraphic Plantin by
Action Typesetting Ltd, Gloucester
Printed and bound in Great Britain by
Butler & Tanner Ltd, Frome, Somerset

Contents

‘

1
Humorous stories and verses

1 Progress

Two men were examining the output of the new computer in their department. Eventually one of them remarked: 'Do you realize it would take 400 men 250 years to make a mistake this big?'

2 Say It Now

Husband with hand on television knob: 'Mary, do you have anything to say before the football season starts?'

3 Instructions Not Clear

The teacher in the mechanics class spoke to one of his pupils: 'I'm putting this rivet in the correct position. When I nod my head, hit it hard with your hammer.' The pupil did, and the teacher woke up the next day in hospital.

4 Modern History

The history teacher had been intoning for the better part of an hour on royal lineage. He droned on, 'Mary followed Edward VI, didn't she?'
CLASS IN UNISON: 'Yes, sir.'
TEACHER: 'And who followed Mary?'
VOICE FROM THE REAR OF THE ROOM: 'Her little lamb.'

’

' 1 Cuts Costs in the Future

LADY: 'This picture makes me look much older than I am.'
PHOTOGRAPHER: 'Well, that will certainly save you the expense of having one taken later on.'

2 He Is Getting Along Well

'How are you getting along at home while your wife's away visiting her mother?'

'Fine. I've reached the height of efficiency. I can put on my socks from either end.'

3 She Was Probably Right

Mother to small son at the table: 'Twenty years from now you'll be telling some girl what a great cook I was. Now be quiet and eat your dinner!'

4 Awkward Age

Father to neighbour: 'My son happens to be at that awkward age. He doesn't know whether to give a girl his seat on the bus – or race her for it.'

5 Attending to Business

Signs of the times – on a parked car in front of the magistrates' court was the sign: 'Solicitor inside attending to business.' When the lawyer returned he found this notice on the car: 'Traffic warden outside attending to business.'

6 Smart Question

'I'm six!' exclaimed a little boy to his neighbour on his birthday.

'Six years old, imagine that,' said the neighbour. 'You're not even as tall as my umbrella!'

'How old is your umbrella?' was the response.

1 Good Endorsement

A young bride tried to cash her husband's pay cheque at a bank. 'You need an endorsement,' the cashier told her.

The bride thought for a moment and then wrote on the back of the cheque: 'My husband is a wonderful man. Sally Johnson.'

2 What He Thinks

MRS SMITH: 'I just can't understand it. The people next door don't have a stereo. They don't have a colour television. She never wears any nice jewellery, and they aren't even members of the tennis club. And to top it all, they drive a 2CV. What do you think?'
MR SMITH: 'I think it's great. They've got money.'

3 That Explains It

After correcting the class's homework, the teacher remarked to one particular boy, 'I just can't understand how one person can make so many mistakes in his work.'

The boy thought for a bit and then commented, 'It wasn't just one person. My Dad helped me.'

4 A Little Different

FATHER: 'Tell me, Susie, how did your test go today?'
SUSIE: 'Well, I did just what Napoleon did.'
FATHER: 'And what's that?'
SUSIE: 'I went down in history.'

5 Didn't Need Help

WAITER: 'May I help you with that soup, sir?'
DINER: 'What do you mean? I don't need any help.'
WAITER: 'Sorry, sir. From the sound I thought you might wish to be dragged ashore.'

6 Smart Lad

The teacher was explaining to his pupils: 'Quite a number of plants and flowers have the prefix "dog". There's the dog-rose and the

' dog-violet, for instance. Can any of you name another?'

There was a silence, and then a happy look appeared on the face of a youngster in the back row.

'Sir,' he asked politely, 'how about collie-flower?'

1 She Didn't Know

The psychiatrist asked the exasperated mother: 'Does your son have a behaviour problem?'

'I don't know . . . I've never seen him behaving,' she replied.

2 Can Figures Lie?

The maths teacher was trying to drive home some truths. 'Figures can't lie,' he declared. 'For instance, if one man can build a house in 12 days, 12 men can build it in one day.'

A puzzled voice interrupted: 'Then 288 men can build it in one hour, 17,280 in one minute, and 1,036,809 in one second.'

While the instructor was still gasping, the ready reckoner went on: 'And if one ship can cross the Atlantic in six days, six ships can cross it in one day. "Figures can't lie," can they?'

3 No Trouble

Once upon a time there were two morons. One of them called the other on the telephone at three o'clock in the morning. 'Hello, is that 4723?'

After a while came the answer, 'No, this is 4724.'

'Well then, sorry to bother you at this time of night.'

'Oh, that's all right. I had to get up to answer the telephone anyway.'

4 Exam Answers

Here are some answers found on primary school exam papers:

'Climate lasts a long time, but the weather is only a few days.'

'A planet is a body of earth surrounded by sky.'

'The feminine of bachelor is lady-in-waiting.'

'A sure-footed animal is an animal that when it kicks does not miss anything.' '

1 Couldn't Fool Him

The chemistry teacher was demonstrating the properties of various acids. 'Now, I am going to drop this silver coin into this glass of acid. Will it dissolve?'

A voice at the rear promptly answered, 'No sir.'

'No?' queried the teacher, a glint in his eye. 'Perhaps you would care to explain to the class why the silver coin won't dissolve.'

The pupil said, 'Because if it would, you wouldn't have dropped it in.'

2 A Warning

A political speaker, warning against higher taxes, said, 'If you don't stop shearing the wool off the sheep that lays the golden egg, you'll pump it dry.'

3 How It Happened

There once was a dachshund so long that he hadn't any notion
Of how long it took to notify his tail of an emotion.
And so it happened, while his eyes were full of woe and sadness,
His little tail went wagging on because of previous gladness.

4 Modern Farming

VISITOR: 'So your son is planning to run the farm when he gets out of college?'

FARMER: 'Well, at least he's beginning to take an interest in it. He's just been showing me where we could have a golf course and how easy it would be to turn the barn into a clubhouse.'

5 The Village Smithy

Beneath the spreading chestnut tree the village smithy snoozes;
No nag, since 1923, has been to him for shoeses.

6 Don't Worry

A baby sardine was happily swimming in the ocean near its mother when it saw its first submarine. The mother quickly reassured her frightened offspring. 'Don't worry, dear. It's just a can of people.'

1 She Remembered

The young husband found his pretty bride weeping when he came home from the office. 'I feel terrible,' she told him. 'When I was pressing your suit, I burned a hole right in the seat of your trousers.'

'Forget it, darling,' he said. 'You must have forgotten that I have an extra pair of trousers for that suit.'

'Oh, I remembered,' answered the bride. 'I cut a piece from them to patch the hole.'

2 Be Careful

A sign in the window of a beauty parlour reads: 'Don't whistle at a girl leaving here. It may be your grandmother.'

3 Good Reason

A boy walked up to the box office at a cinema one Wednesday afternoon and handed the cashier the money for a ticket.

'It's only one o'clock,' she said to him. 'Why aren't you in school?'

'Oh, it's all right,' he said, 'I've got the measles.'

4 Thoughtful Opinion

Two goats wandered into an alley behind a cinema, looking for their dinner. They found a can of film, which one of them devoured, along with the can.

'How was it?' his companion asked.

'I think the book was better,' he replied.

5 Psychiatrist

Two publishers ran into each other at the door of the psychiatrist's office.

'Hello,' said one. 'Are you coming or going?'

'If I knew that,' replied the other, 'I wouldn't be here.'

6 Of Course

'How did I get here?' the baby ear of corn asked its mother.

'The stalk brought you.'

1 Thoughtful

Teacher to a class of small children: 'Will all those who think they are stupid stand up.'

For a moment no one got up, then one little boy stood.

'Billy,' said the teacher, 'do you think you are stupid?'

'No, Miss,' was the answer. 'I just didn't like to see you standing up by yourself!'

2 They Don't Live There

'I like the scenery around here,' commented a tourist to a local Cornishman, 'but most of the people are so strange.'

'That's true,' replied the Cornishman, 'but most of them go home at the end of the summer.'

3 Very Clever

'Looks like you've got a clever dog there,' remarked a friend.

'Clever? All I have to tell him is "Are you coming or aren't you?" And he either comes or he doesn't.'

4 There Is a Difference

MR GREEN: 'My wife is very poetic; she gets up at sunrise and says, "Lo, the morn!"'

MR GREY: 'What! You lucky man. My wife gets up and says, "Mow the lawn!"'

5 It Always Does

PROFESSOR: 'What happens when the human body is immersed in water?'

STUDENT: 'The telephone rings.'

6 Next Question

TEACHER: 'Tommy, name five things that contain milk.'

TOMMY: 'Butter, cheese, ice cream and two cows.'

1 Not Always

It was a wise youngster who, on being asked, 'What is the chief end of man?' replied, 'The end that's got the head on.'

2 Wanted to Be Ready

BOBBY: 'Mum, when we have guests for tea today, do I have to eat my cake with a fork?'
MUM: 'Yes, indeed you do.'
BOBBY: 'Well, have you got enough cake so I could practise with a fork for a while before they come?'

3 Of Course Not

'Yes, I used to shoot tigers in the Highlands,' asserted the big game hunter, boastfully.
   'But there are no tigers in the Highlands,' protested a listener.
   'Certainly not!' exclaimed the hunter. 'I got them all!'

4 He Did

HEAD COOK: 'Didn't I tell you to notice when the soup boiled over?'
ASSISTANT: 'I did – it was at half-past ten.'

5 One Answer

TEACHER: 'Boys, who is man's noblest friend?'
TIMMY: 'The hot dog – it feeds the hand that bites it.'

6 Hard Worker

BOSS: 'How is it that you're only carrying one sack when the other hands are carrying two?'
WORKER: 'Well, maybe they're just too lazy to make two trips like I do.'

7 A Five Star Restaurant

A motorist and his wife stopped at an unimpressive café. Both ordered tea, the wife adding, 'And be sure my cup is absolutely 'clean!' A second waitress appeared a few minutes later. 'Here they are,' she said. 'Which one gets the clean cup?'

1 Great Shot

A group of first-year astronomy students had their first class in the observation laboratory one evening. The lecturer went to the telescope and began to make an observation. Just then a star fell.

'That was a fine shot,' one of the students said. 'Why, he hardly had time to take aim.'

2 Different Meaning

'Mother, what does "apt" mean?' little Billy asked one day after returning from school.

'Why, dear, it means "clever, quick to learn". Why do you ask?'

'Oh, nothing much,' said Billy airily. 'The teacher just told me today I was apt to flunk things.'

3 Be Careful

Little Johnny was in one of his very bad and disobedient moods. In answer to his mother's remonstrations that he behave himself, he said: 'Give me a pound and I'll be good.'

'Give you a pound!' She scolded: 'Why Johnny, you shouldn't be good for a pound, you should be good for nothing – like your father.'

4 He Needs Help

PATIENT: 'Doctor, I can't remember anything from one minute to the next. I'm worried.'

PSYCHIATRIST: 'Just how long has this been going on?'

PATIENT: 'How long has what been going on?'

5 Hard Question

Little Bobby took a long look at the old man and asked, 'Were you on the Ark, Grandpa, when the flood came?'

'No, certainly not,' replied his grandfather.

'Well then, why weren't you drowned?'

1 Too Often Neglected

When a small boy saw a Bible, not too recently dusted, lying on a shelf in his home, he asked his mother whose book it was.

'It is God's book,' she said.

'Well,' the boy commented, 'don't you think we should return it? Nobody seems to read it round here!'

2 The Ten Commandments

A young woman was sending the old family Bible to her brother in a distant town. The clerk at the post office counter examined the package carefully and enquired whether it contained anything breakable.

'Nothing but the Ten Commandments,' was her quick reply.

3 Time Flies

Frustrated diner: 'You tell me you're the same fellow who took my order. Somehow, I expected a much older waiter.'

4 His Viewpoint

The proud parents took their little boy to church for the first time. When the members of the choir entered in their flowing, white robes, the child whispered: 'Look, they're all going to get their hair cut.'

5 It Makes You Lose Weight

The secretary ran into a friend at a lunchtime restaurant and saw that the friend was eating a cottage cheese salad.

'Are you trying to lose weight?' the secretary asked.

'Oh, no,' the friend replied. 'I'm on a low salary diet.'

6 Just Remember

If life may seem to trick you,
And give you the boot,
Just remember that there's only one thing can lick you,
And that's the guy inside your suit.

1 What He Pays For

The balding middle-aged man asked his barber, 'Why charge me the full price for cutting my hair — there's so little of it?'

'Well,' said the barber, 'actually I make little charge for cutting it. What you're really paying for is my searching for it!'

2 Hard Decision

BARBER: 'You want your hair parted exactly in the middle, sir?'
CUSTOMER: 'That's what I said, didn't I?'
BARBER: 'Then I'll have to pull one out, sir. You have five hairs.'

3 Smart Hens

The young married woman and her husband had moved to the country to live, and she was on her first visit back to the city.

'So, you like country life,' her father said. 'Are your hens good layers?'

'They're experts,' she replied. 'They haven't laid a bad egg yet.'

4 Good Question

Dismayed by the size of the St Bernard dog given him for his birthday, the little boy asked, 'Is he for me, or am I for him?'

5 His Wife Has a Problem Also

'Well, John, how does it feel to be a grandfather?'

'Oh, it's good news, of course, but I'll have to get used to the idea of being married to a grandmother!'

6 That's Different

'Happiness,' claimed the philosopher, 'is the pursuit of something, not the catching of it.'

'Have you ever,' interrupted a listener, 'chased the last bus on a rainy night?'

❮ 1 Why Hold Back?

LADY: 'I'll give you a pound – not because you deserve it, but because it pleases me to do so.'

TRAMP: 'Thank you, ma'am, but why not make it a fiver and really enjoy yourself?'

2 Good Question

A primary school class were visiting a museum of Egyptology with their teacher. 'Why,' one little boy wanted to know, 'are there so many mummies and no daddies?'

3 Anything to Help

The diner was agitated because the waiter had brought him no spoon with his cup and saucer.

'This coffee,' he said pointedly, 'is going to be pretty hot to stir with my fingers.'

The waiter reddened and beat a hasty retreat to the kitchen. He returned shortly with another cup of coffee.

'This one isn't so hot, sir,' he beamed.

4 Ready to Go

The football club manager was dejected because his team was losing badly. He looked down the bench at his substitutes and yelled: 'Jones, go in there and get ferocious!'

Jones, who hadn't been on the field all season, jumped up with a start and said, 'OK, boss. He's the striker, right?'

5 One More Would Be Enough

'Another bite like that, young lady,' a mother told her young daughter, 'and you'll have to leave this table.'

'Another bite like that and I'll be finished,' was the little one's reply.

6 In Doubt

CUSTOMER: 'Remember that cheese you sold me yesterday?'

GROCER: 'Yes, madam.' ❯

‘   CUSTOMER: 'Did you say it was imported or deported from Switzerland?'

1 It's Easy

The golfer stepped up to the tee and drove off. The ball sailed down the fairway, leaped on to the green and rolled into the hole. He threw his club into the air with excitement.

'Have you suddenly gone crazy?' asked his wife, who was trying to learn the game.

'I just did a hole in one!' yelled the golfer, a gleam of delight in his eyes.

'Did you?' his wife asked placidly. 'Do it again, dear – I didn't see you.'

2 He Was Certain

Father was sitting in his armchair one evening when his little son came in and showed him a new penknife, which he said he had found in the street.

'Are you sure it was lost?' the father enquired.

'Of course it was lost! I saw the man looking for it!' replied the youngster.

3 Only the Top

Two sailors, at sea for the first time, were looking out over the mighty ocean. Said one, 'That's the most water I ever saw.'

The other replied, 'You ain't seen nothin' yet. That's just the top of it.'

4 Slow to Learn

The junior sales manager complained to his wife of aches and pains. Neither could account for his trouble. Arriving home one night from work, he informed her, 'I finally discovered why I've been feeling so miserable. We got some ultra-modern office furniture two weeks ago, and I just learned today that I've been sitting in the wastebasket.' ’

1 Good Reason

'There are a lot of twins being born these days,' said Smith, looking up from his newspaper.

'Naturally,' said his companion and added, 'The shape the world is in nowadays, the poor kids are afraid to come into it alone.'

2 Good Advice

A speaker at a luncheon club gave a tremendous talk and received a standing ovation. The president was so impressed that he said to the speaker, 'Everyone here is delighted. Won't you please say a few more words, since we have ten minutes left?'

So the speaker said, 'Once there was a little baby cabbage who said to his mother, "Mummy, I'm worried about something. As I sit in this row of cabbages and grow and grow day after day, how will I know when to stop growing?"

'"The rule to follow," said the mamma cabbage, "is to quit when you are a head."'

3 Stop Acting

The teacher seemed greatly irritated at the action of one of his pupils. 'Listen, boy,' he exclaimed, 'are you the teacher of this class?'

'No, sir, I'm not,' answered the lad boldly.

'Well, then, stop acting like a fool!'

4 A Young Salesman

A youngster walked into a bank the other day to open an account with £25. The cashier gave him a benign smile and asked how he had accumulated so much money.

'Selling Christmas cards,' said the lad.

'Well, you've done very well. Sold them to lots of people, obviously.'

'No,' said the little boy proudly, 'I sold all of them to one family – their dog bit me.'

1 That's Different

Two Irish labourers were hired to paint some flagpoles. One fellow stood on the other's shoulders and reached up as far as he could. The foreman passed by and wanted to know what they were doing. 'We've got to measure how high the pole is so we can work out how much paint we'll need.'

The foreman said, 'Nonsense. Take the flagpole down and lay it on the ground. Then you can measure it.'

One of the labourers said, 'A lot you know. We want to find out how high it is, not how long it is.'

2 In the Old Days

Bothered by the frequent tea breaks and other interruptions in the modern working day, the veteran plumber said, 'Back in the days when I was taught my trade, we never did any of this. After we'd installed two lengths of pipe, our foreman would turn on the water. If we couldn't keep ahead of it, we'd get the sack.'

3 Real Problem

A doctor recommended one of his patients to lose about 3 stone. The doctor's instructions were to run five miles a day for the next 100 days. The overweight patient called the doctor exactly 100 days later and complained that he was unhappy with the weight-loss programme.

'But haven't you lost the weight?' questioned the doctor.

'Certainly I did,' the patient replied. 'But I'm 500 miles from home!'

4 Correct Answer

TEACHER: 'Name three collective nouns.'
PUPIL: 'Dustpan, waste paper basket and vacuum cleaner.'

5 Cheaper

Two middle-aged men were discussing a mutual friend. Said one, 'Poor old John seems to be living in the past.'

'Well, why not?' replied the other man. 'It's a lot cheaper.'

‘ 1 He Couldn't Sleep

A man booked a room in a hotel, and the receptionist warned that the guest in the next room was very nervous. When the man went to his room, he thoughtlessly threw his shoe down very hard. Then he remembered the poor nervous guest in the next room, so he laid the other shoe down very gently. He went to bed, and about two hours later he heard a rap at the door. He asked who it was, and the nervous man said: 'For heaven's sake throw that other shoe down, will you?'

2 It Was Worse Then

The kindly old lady was much impressed with the street beggar. 'Oh, you poor man!' she exclaimed. 'It must be dreadful to be lame. But you know, it could be worse. I think it would be much worse if you were blind!'

'You're tellin' me, lady,' responded the beggar. 'When I was blind, all I ever got from people was pennies.'

3 No Time

Little Alice came into the house all bedraggled and weeping.

'My goodness,' cried her mother, 'what a sight you are! How on earth did it happen?'

'I'm s-so s-sorry, Mummy, but I fell into a puddle of mud.'

'What! With your new dress on?'

'Y-y-yes, I didn't have time to change it.'

4 He Certainly Is

'Billy's very conceited, isn't he?'

'I'll say. Did you know that on his last birthday he sent a note of congratulation to his parents?'

5 His Technique

A man with middle-age spread was discussing his tennis technique.

'My brain barks out a command to my body: "Run forward speedily. Start right away. Slam the ball gracefully over the net."' ’

'And then what happens?' his friend enquired.

'And then,' the out-of-shape fellow replied, 'my body stops and says: "Who, me?"'

1 It Helps

Young husband to his neighbour: 'My wife is a good cook. She can prepare the best meal you ever thaw!'

2 Good Reason

FOREMAN: 'Why are you late?'

WORKER: 'I had car trouble.'

FOREMAN: 'What's wrong with your car?'

WORKER: 'I was late getting into it.'

3 He Knows Them All

The parents were listening to their eight-year-old practising away on his trumpet while their dog loudly howled at his side.

Finally, the father said: 'Johnnie, why don't you play something the dog doesn't know?'

4 Meets the Test

TEACHER: 'Bobby, if you don't settle down and become more serious, you'll never grow up to be a very responsible man.'

BOBBY: 'But I'm a responsible boy even now. Every time something happens at home, Mum always tells me I'm responsible.'

5 Wrong Question

POLITICIAN: 'Well, dear, I've been re-elected!'

WIFE: 'Honestly?'

POLITICIAN: 'I don't see that there's any need for you to bring that up.'

❛ 1 Real Talent

'My grandfather plays the piano by ear,' said the boy.
  'Well, if we must boast – my grandfather fiddles with his beard,' was the other child's ready reply.

2 No Rest

'As maintenance of this churchyard is becoming increasingly difficult and expensive, it will be appreciated if parishioners will cut the grass around their own graves.'

Notice in an Essex newspaper

3 Advice

'I saw a psychiatrist today about my memory lapses.'
  'Oh really? What did he say?'
  'He said I'd have to pay my bill in advance.'

4 He Knew It

A little boy was talking to a friend about the recent fire in their school. 'I knew it was going to happen – we'd been practising for it all year.'

5 She Asked First

A lady with her cheque book in a muddle phoned her bank for help.
  'What balance have you got?' asked the bank clerk.
  'I asked you first,' replied the caller.

6 It Helps

A recent bride bragged to another newly-wed, 'I have my husband eating out of my hand.'
  Replied her friend: 'Cuts down the washing up, doesn't it?' ❜

1 Grocer's Mistake

'I baked a sponge cake for you, darling,' the young bride announced, 'but it didn't turn out quite right. I think I bought the wrong kind of sponge in the supermarket.'

2 A Big Job

'I'm sorry I'm late, Mum,' said ten-year-old Jimmy as he rushed home from school. 'We were making a science display, and I had to stay to finish the universe.'

3 He Sneezed a Sneeze

I sneezed a sneeze into the air;
It fell to earth I knew not where.
But hard and cold were the looks of those
In whose vicinity I snoze.

4 Quick to Learn

A poodle and a cocker spaniel met in the park. The poodle said, 'My name's Fifi, what's yours?'
  Replied the spaniel, 'I think it's Down Boy.'

5 Speaks from Experience

The youngster told his little brother he could be spared a lot of misery by refusing to spell his first word. 'The minute you spell "cat", you're trapped,' he said. 'After that the words get harder and harder.'

6 Tried to Help

Two Cubs, whose younger brother had fallen into the lake, rushed home to mother with tears in their eyes.
  'We try to give him artificial respiration,' one of them sobbed, 'but he keeps getting up and walking away.'

1 Not Too Fussy

EMPLOYER: 'I'm sorry I can't hire you, but I just couldn't find enough work to keep you busy.'
APPLICANT: 'You'd be surprised how little it takes.'

2 Almost Perfect

'How're you getting along with your new second-hand car?' Mr Smith asked.

'Well,' said Mr Jones, 'there's only one part of it that doesn't make a noise, and that's the horn.'

3 Very Careful

A museum curator said to the removals man: 'Be very careful when you carry this vase, it's 2,000 years old.'

'You can count on me,' the removals man said. 'I'll carry it just as if it were new.'

4 Not Necessary

One business partner to the other, on a fishing trip: 'We forgot to lock the safe!'

'What's the problem? We're both here, aren't we?'

5 Think Before You Speak

At a dinner party, a shy young man kept trying to think of something nice to say to the hostess. At last he saw his chance when the hostess turned to him and said, 'What a small appetite you have, Mr Brown.'

'Sitting next to you,' he remarked gallantly, 'would cause anyone to lose his appetite.'

6 A Little Late

A second-floor tenant called to the occupant of the flat below and shouted: 'If you don't stop playing those drums, I'll go crazy.'

'I think it's too late,' came the reply. 'I stopped playing them an hour ago.'

1 Meant Well

People do not always mean what they say. A kind-hearted woman raised money to send to an area where there had been a disaster. It took her longer to get the money together than she had anticipated, and she feared it would be too late arriving. So she sent this note with the contribution: 'We hope the suffering is not all over.'

2 No Mozart

NEIGHBOUR: 'Where's your little sister, Linda?'
LINDA: 'In the house playing a duet . . . I finished first.'

3 Do You Think?

At night, before I sleep, I lie
And think and think, and wonder why.

Why tables have legs, and cannot walk;
Why pitchers have mouths, and cannot talk;
Why needles have eyes, and cannot wink;
Why pins have heads, and cannot think;
Why houses have wings, and cannot fly;
Why flowers have beds, and cannot lie;
Why clocks have hands, and cannot write;
Why combs have teeth, and cannot bite.

I think and think till I cannot sleep,
And have to end up counting sheep!

1 It Changed Him

A movie executive, famous for his long after-dinner speeches, now expresses himself with brevity. Asked to explain his change of tack, he replied: 'It was a remark I overheard. During a pause in one of my speeches, one man said to another, "What follows this speaker?" The other man said, "Wednesday."'

2 Be Fair and Help

The burglars tied and gagged the cashier after extracting the combination to the safe, and herded the other employees into a separate room under guard. After they rifled the safe and were about to leave, the cashier made desperate pleading noises through the gag. Moved by curiosity, one of the burglars loosened the gag.

'Please,' whispered the cashier, 'take the books too. I'm £6,500 short.'

3 She Loves Gardening

The man with the permanent stoop said to his sympathetic neighbour: 'My wife loves gardening. I don't think there's anything she'd rather see me do.'

4 Hold It

'If anything goes wrong with this experiment,' said the chemistry teacher, 'we and the laboratory will be blown sky-high. Come a little closer, so you can follow me.'

5 He Likes It

WAITRESS: 'This is your fifth cup, sir. You must really like the coffee.'

DINER: 'I certainly do. That's why I'm willing to drink all this water to get a little of it.'

6 Correct

From a schoolboy's exam paper: 'The Matterhorn was a horn blown by the ancients when anything was the matter.'

1 How Else?

An office manager was asking a female applicant if she had any unusual talents. She said she had won several prizes in crossword puzzle and slogan-writing contests.

'Sounds good,' the manager told her, 'but we want somebody who can be smart during office hours.'

'Oh,' said the applicant, 'that *was* during office hours.'

2 My Kingdom for a Horse

The critic said to the sculptor, 'It's a fine statue, all right, but isn't that a rather odd position for a general to assume?'

'Maybe so,' said the sculptor, 'but I was halfway finished when the committee ran out of money and couldn't afford a horse for him.'

3 He Remembered

The will of a wealthy man was being read, and the relatives all listened expectantly, especially his playboy nephew. Finally, the lawyer read: 'And to my nephew, John, whom I promised not to forget in my will − "Hi there, John."'

4 An Idea

Turkey addressing farmyard flock: 'Here's the plan. We go on hunger strike so that by Christmas we're nothing but skin and bones.'

5 Easier Then

It was the minute of rest between the ninth and tenth rounds, and the battered fighter sat on his stool, his seconds working furiously over his bleeding face.

'I think he's got you whipped,' said his manager in disgust.

'Yeah,' agreed the pugilist, gazing dizzily through nearly closed eyes. 'I should have got him in the first round when he was by himself.'

‘ 1 Remarkable

SLOW WAITER: 'This coffee is imported from Brazil.'
EXASPERATED CUSTOMER: 'My goodness – and it's still warm!'

2 Looking Ahead

Weary father of a five-year-old to wife: 'Talk! Talk! Thank goodness in a few years he'll be a teenager and we won't be able to communicate with him.'

3 What He Observed

'Johnnie, there is a wonderful example in the life of an ant,' the father pointed out to his youngster. 'Every day the ant goes to work, and works all day. Every day the ant is busy, and in the end what happens?'

Unimpressed, the lad replied, 'Someone steps on him.'

4 Have Faith

A preacher who was in the habit of writing his sermons out carefully found himself at church one Sunday morning without his manuscript.

'As I have forgotten my notes,' he said at the beginning of his sermon, 'I will have to rely on the Lord for guidance. Next week I shall come better prepared.'

5 Not Clear

The cookery teacher was explaining a recipe to her class and said, 'When the mixture comes to the boil, add one tablespoon of milk.'

One of the girls asked, 'Is that level or heaped?'

6 Not Selfish

PROUD DAD: 'Yes, son, I am a self-made man.'
SON: 'That's what I like about you, Dad. You take the blame for everything.' ’

1 Come Early

Notice in a parish magazine: 'Come to the morning service early if you want a good back seat!'

2 Opinion

WOMAN: 'Aren't those chimes beautiful? Such harmony! So enchanting!'

MAN: 'You'll have to speak louder. Those confounded bells are making such a racket I can't hear you!'

3 Modern

PARENT: 'Isn't this toy rather complex for a small child?'

ASSISTANT: 'Oh, but this is an educational toy designed to provide the child with a means of adjusting to today's world. No matter which way the child assembles this toy it's wrong.'

4 Amazed

REPORTER INTERVIEWING CENTENARIAN: 'How do you feel when you get up in the morning?'

CENTENARIAN: 'Amazed.'

5 That's Different

The company's personnel department was checking on a job applicant's list of references.

'How long did this person work for you?' a former employer was asked.

'About six hours,' was the reply.

'But he informed us he'd been working for you a long time.'

'Oh, yes,' the ex-employer answered tersely, 'he's *been* here for four years.'

6 If You Ain't Sure

The teacher was trying to teach her class good grammar.

'You should never say, "I seen him do it,"' she told them.

'Yeah,' piped a voice from the back of the room. 'Especially if you ain't sure he done it.'

1 It Was Worth It

A fisherman was taken to court for catching ten more salmon than his licence allowed. 'Guilty or not guilty?' asked the magistrate.

'Guilty,' said the sportsman.

'£25 and costs,' remarked the judge.

After cheerfully paying the fine, the fisherman made one request: 'And now I'd respectfully like to ask for several copies of the court record to show my friends.'

2 The Worst Part

Two little girls were discussing the subject of piggy banks.

'I think it's childish to save money that way,' Mary said.

'I do too,' Annie replied. 'And I also believe that it encourages children to become misers.'

'And that's not the worst of it,' Mary exclaimed. 'It turns parents into bank robbers!'

1 Is That Clear?

The portly sales manager was getting ready to leave his doctor's surgery after a routine examination.

'Here,' said the doctor, 'follow this diet, and I want to see three-quarters of you back here for a check-up in three months.'

2 Not Easy

Struggling with the English language, the foreigner was completely frustrated by the reasoning behind the pronunciation of words like tough, bough and though. He gave up when he read this local newspaper headline: 'Bazaar Pronounced Success.'

3 He Knew

The lion tamer walked into a cage of lions at the circus, and everyone in the audience was nervous except one grey-haired man.

'I know what it feels like,' he explained. 'I drive a school bus myself.'

4 A Big Star

A teenage girl was talking to a friend about a new pop singer she'd heard. 'I know he's going to be a big star,' she said confidently. 'My father can't stand him.'

5 What He Would Do

The teacher asked her students to write an essay, explaining what they would do if they each won £1 million on the pools. Every pupil except Peter began writing. He just sat in his chair twiddling his thumbs.

At the end of the lesson the teacher collected the papers. Peter's sheet was still blank.

'What's the meaning of this?' the teacher asked. 'All the others have written two pages or more, but you've done nothing!'

'Well,' replied Peter, 'If I had that much money, that's exactly what I'd do – nothing.'

‘ 1 Very Quiet

Man to friend: 'We're going to have a quiet Christmas this year –
I'm giving the wife everything she's been dropping hints about.'

2 Helpful

'Yes, I'll give you a job. You can start by sweeping the floor.'
  'But I'm a university graduate!'
  'Get a broom and I'll show you how, then.'

3 His Opinion

'Well, sir,' asked the musician, 'what do you think of my
compositions?'
  'What do I think of them?' answered the critic. 'Well, they will be
played when Gounod, Beethoven and Wagner are forgotten.'
  'Really?'
  'Yes, but not before.'

4 A Nuisance

WOMAN: 'I want to return this parrot my husband bought me.'
SHOPKEEPER: 'Doesn't it speak?'
WOMAN: 'On the contrary. It never stops interrupting me.'

5 Can't Mistake Him

FRED: 'What kind of fellow is Jim? I haven't met him.'
JOE: 'Well, if you see two blokes talking anywhere and one of them
  looks bored to death, the other one is bound to be Jim.'

6 Only Once

HOUSEWIFE: 'Has anyone offered you work?'
TRAMP: 'Only once, ma'am. Other than that, I've met with nothing
  but kindness.' ’

❛ 1 Dejected

'Charlie, why don't you play golf with Ted any more?' asked the wife.

'Would you play golf with a chap who moved the ball with his foot when you weren't watching?' he said.

'Well, no,' admitted the wife.

'And neither will Ted,' replied the dejected husband.

2 Hard Work

A tired-looking man dragged himself through his front door and slumped into an easy chair.

'Busy day at the office, dear?' his wife asked sympathetically.

'Terrible,' he sighed. 'The computer broke down in the middle of the afternoon, and we all had to think for the rest of the day.'

3 New Endings

A primary school teacher gave her class the first half of various proverbs and asked the children to complete them. Here are some of the results:

Don't count your chickens – before you cook them.

Don't put all your eggs – in the microwave.

All's fair in – football.

People who live in glass houses – shouldn't take off their clothes.

If at first you don't succeed – go and play.

All work and no play – is disgusting.

He who laughs last – didn't understand the joke.

The race is not to the swift – but to the finish line.

Two heads are – funny looking.

A stitch in time saves – your pants.

Better late than – missing school.

The grass is always greener – than the cows.

Clothes make – people decent.

Do unto others – like you don't do to yourself.

We have nothing to fear but – we're still scared. ❜

1 Trouble Ahead

'And what did my little boy do today?' the working mother asked.

'I played postman,' he replied. 'I delivered real letters to all the houses in the street. I found them tied with pink ribbon in your bottom drawer.'

2 Helpful

Said an anxious wife as she watched her husband fishing in a bucket of water in the middle of the living room, 'I'd take him to a psychiatrist, but we really need the fish.'

3 Getting Old

You wonder if you're getting old?
My girl, the test is this:
When people start to call you 'Ma'am'
Who used to call you 'Miss'.

' 1 Why Not?

LORRY DRIVER AT PULL-IN: 'I'll have hard bacon, cold eggs, undercooked sausages, a stale bread roll and weak tea.'
WAITRESS: 'I can't serve you that, sir!'
LORRY DRIVER: 'Why not? You did the last time I was here.'

2 Be Careful

'John,' complained the wife, 'I think I should be paid for doing housework.'
'Of course dear, but I only need you to come in on Fridays.'

3 No One to Blame

A worker on a building site opened his lunchbox, looked in and growled, 'Cheese sandwiches! Cheese sandwiches! Always cheese sandwiches for lunch!'
A fellow worker sitting close by overheard him and asked, 'Why don't you ask your wife to make some other kind?'
'Wife?' said the man. 'Who's married? I make these myself.'

4 Modern Times

A modern mother and her young son were shopping in a supermarket. The child, trying to help, picked up a package and brought it to her. 'No, no, darling,' protested the mother, 'put it back. You have to cook that.'

5 Not Fair

Two fishermen sitting on a bridge, their lines in the water, made a bet as to who'd catch the first fish. One got a bite and became so excited that he fell off the bridge.
'Oh, well,' said the other, 'if you're going to dive for them, the bet's off!' '

‘ 1 Handling a Problem

The famous actor John Barrymore was playing in a Broadway theatre, and a very noisy person in one of the boxes was directing remarks to the stage to show everyone that he knew Barrymore. Finally, in the middle of a scene, Barrymore walked down to the footlights and said, 'Ladies and gentlemen, please excuse my friend in the box. I haven't seen him for a long time. Now you understand why!'

2 Of Course Not

DOCTOR: 'You're overweight again, Mrs Fuller. You haven't been keeping strictly to that diet I gave you.'
MRS FULLER: 'Well, no, doctor. After all, I don't want to starve to death just for the sake of living a little bit longer.'

3 No Substitute

'Sorry we don't have potted geraniums,' the girl in the florist's said, and then added helpfully, 'How about some nice African violets?'

'No,' replied the man sadly. 'It was geraniums my wife told me to water while she was gone.'

4 One Explanation

TEACHER: 'What is the difference between electricity and lightning?'
PUPIL: 'We don't have to pay for lightning.'

5 Definitely Maybe

The boss, leaving the office, was instructing his new secretary on what to say while he was out.

'I may be back before lunch,' he told her. 'And then again, I may not. I may not be back until tomorrow morning.'

'Yes, sir,' the secretary said. 'Is that definite?' ’

1 Too Late

The young couple had had their first quarrel, and for several hours neither would speak to the other. Finally the husband decided to give in.

'Please speak to me, dear,' he said. 'I'll admit I was wrong and you were right.'

'It won't do any good,' sobbed the bride, 'I've changed my mind.'

2 Not Quite Certain

OFFICE CLERK: 'Please, sir, I think you're wanted on the phone.'
EMPLOYER: 'You think! Don't you know?'
OFFICE CLERK: 'Well, sir, the voice at the other end said, "Hello, is that you, you old idiot?"'

3 Progress

The proud father and mother had given their son a bicycle and were watching him as he rode round the block.

On his first trip around he called: 'Look, Mum, no hands!'

On the second trip: 'Look, Mum, no feet!'

And his third time: 'Look, Mum, no teeth!'

4 Just Remember

'Son,' a father told his growing boy, 'just remember one thing: I know a lot more about being young than you know about being old.'

5 It's Easy to Make

TEACHER: 'If I take a potato and divide it into two parts, then into four parts, and each of the four parts into two pairs, what would I have?'
LITTLE EMILY: 'Potato salad.'

6 One Too Many

'Daddy!' cried the boy.

'One more question, then,' sighed the tired father.

'How far is it,' enquired the tot, 'between to and fro?'

1 Golf

'I'd move heaven and earth to break 100,' announced the novice golfer as he banged away in a sand bunker.

'Try heaven,' advised his partner. 'I think you've already moved enough earth.'

2 Frustrated

The joke you just told isn't funny one bit.
It is pointless and dull, wholly lacking in wit.
It's so old and so stale it's beginning to smell.
(Besides, it's the one I was planning to tell.)

3 A Tale

FRED: 'Have you heard the story of the peacock?'
JOE: 'No, I haven't.'
FRED: 'It's a beautiful tale.'

4 Right

TEACHER: 'Can anyone tell me what the highest form of animal life is?'
SUSAN: 'Yes, the giraffe.'

5 For Reasons of Health

'It's not that I really cheat,' the golfer explained, 'it's just that I play for my health, and the low score makes me feel better.'

6 Passed His English Course

'Whom are you?' said he, for he had been to night school.

George Ade

7 Forget the Age

'You were swindled over this Rembrandt. The picture isn't 50 years old.'

'I don't care about age so long as it's a genuine Rembrandt.'

1 Must Have Been to Manchester

'It's nice to be back from holiday. It rained most of the time.'
 'It couldn't have been too bad. That's a nice tan you have.'
 'That's not a tan. That's rust.'

2 Good Try

SPORTS CAR DRIVER: 'But I wasn't doing 100!'
MOTORWAY POLICEMAN: 'Maybe not. However, I'm going to give
 you this ticket as first prize for trying.'

3 Correct

JERRY: 'John's wife always laughs at his jokes.'
JUDY: 'They must be pretty clever.'
JERRY: 'No – she is.'

4 Willing

Want ad: 'Lovely kitten desires position as companion to little girl.
Will also do light mouse work.'

5 Nothing Really Wrong

A small boy in a department store was standing near the escalator
watching the moving handrail.
 'Something wrong, son?' enquired a sales assistant.
 'No,' replied the boy. 'Just waiting for my chewing gum to come
back.'

6 It Helps

'I drink from twelve to fifteen cups of coffee every day.'
 'Doesn't it keep you awake?'
 'Well, it helps.'

7 Can't Win

Calling my wife on the telephone is a task that makes me dizzy.
When the line is clear, she isn't home, and when she's home, it's
busy.

' **1 Very Cautious**

The young lion tamer was being interviewed on television.

'I understand your father also was a lion tamer,' said the announcer.

'Yes, indeed he was,' said the young man.

'And do you actually put your head in the lion's mouth?'

'I only did it once,' said the young man. 'To look for Dad.'

2 Honest

As the three ladies picked up the concert programme, each put on a pair of glasses.

'Of course, I really need mine only for close reading,' said one.

'I wear mine only when the light is poor,' said the second.

The third was honest. 'I rarely wear mine,' she said, 'except when I want to see.'

3 Insult

As Smith was driving down a country road, a pig ran out in front of the car and was run over.

The farmer saw the accident and was understandably annoyed. He vigorously protested his loss.

Smith was apologetic and said he would replace the animal.

The farmer smiled wryly at Smith and said, 'You flatter yourself.'

4 Couldn't Do It

ANGRY GUIDE: 'Why didn't you shoot that tiger?'

TIMID HUNTER: 'He didn't have the right kind of expression on his face for a rug.'

5 Her Wishes

Just give me a man with a million or two,
Or one who is handsome would happily do.
A dashing young fellow is swell any day,
Or one who is famous would suit me okay.
But if the man shortage should get any worse,
Go back to the very first line in this verse.

'

' 1 Nagging

'My husband,' explained Mrs Smith, 'is an efficiency expert for a large company.'

'Imagine that,' said Mrs Jones. 'But tell me, what does an efficiency expert do?'

Mrs Smith gave the matter some thought and said, 'Well, I'm not sure I can describe it exactly. When I do it, he calls it nagging.'

2 Logical

An artist was spending his holiday in an out-of-the way little town. He entered the general store and asked if they carried camel hair brushes.

'No, sir. We don't,' replied the shopkeeper. 'Y'see, we never have no call for them. Nobody in these parts seems to keep camels.'

3 Quit Living Normally

The doctor examined the patient thoroughly and asked, 'Have you been living a normal life?'

'Yes doctor,' the patient replied.

'Well, you'll have to cut it out for a while.'

4 Jumping to a Conclusion

The flying instructor, having delivered a lecture on parachuting, concluded: 'And if it doesn't open, and then your reserve 'chute doesn't open either – well, gentlemen, that's what is known as "jumping to a conclusion".'

5 Wrong Number

VOICE (DURING A TELEPHONE CONVERSATION): 'And tell me, how are you feeling this morning?'

ANSWER: 'Oh, just fine.'

VOICE: 'I think I must have the wrong number!' '

1 It Depends

'Is it true,' the reporter asked the explorer, 'that wild animals in the jungle will not harm you if you carry a torch?'

'It all depends,' said the explorer, 'on how fast you carry it.'

2 Efficient Service

Shoe department manager: 'Yes, we have quite a selection of loafers. I'll see if I can get one to wait on you.'

3 Under Oath

'What is your age?' asked the barrister in court. 'And remember, you are under oath.'

'I am twenty-one and some months,' the woman answered.

'How many months?'

'One hundred and eight.'

4. Only the Teachers

A teacher described the excitement when school broke up for the holidays. 'There was foot stamping, wall banging and all sorts of rejoicing,' he said.

'Wild, eh?' said the listener.

'Yes,' said the teacher, 'and that was only in the staff room.'

5 The Next Step

Teacher's report: 'Your son excels in initiative, group integration, responsiveness and activity participation. Now he should learn to read and write.'

6 Like Most of Us

GOLFER: 'I'm certainly not playing the game I used to play.'
DISGUSTED CADDY: 'What game was that, sir?'

1 Don't Try It

HUSBAND: 'The bank has returned your cheque.'
WIFE: 'Isn't that wonderful! What shall we buy with it this time?'

2 That's Different

COUNTRY RESIDENT: 'It's lovely to wake up in the morning and hear the leaves whispering outside your window.'
TOWN DWELLER: 'It's all right to hear the leaves whisper, but I never could stand hearing the grass mown.'

3 They Made a Sale

'Were there any new orders while I was out?' the shop manager asked his new assistant.

'Only one,' she replied. 'Two men ordered me to put up my hands while they took the safe.'

4 A Sad Poem

A little boy at the end of his rope,
Facing a towel, water and soap.

5 A Poem on Time

'I haven't time!' These idle words are not exactly true,
Because I always find the time for things I want to do.

6 Worth Knowing

Here's a fact that's worth the knowing,
So treasure and mark it well;
When the mind is through with growing,
Then the head begins to swell.

7 A Real Tragedy

Of tragedies both great and small
Within the reach of my recall,
There's none of them can ever par,
The first little dent in my new car.

(1 It's Hard Work

The man who goes on a fishing holiday usually gets a lot of additional exercise when he gets home. He has to stretch his arms to their full extent every time he meets a friend to show him the size of the fish that got away.

2 Failure of Parental Discipline

It used to be that Dad could exert a stern code of discipline. Then the electric razor took away his razor strop, central heating took away his woodshed, and tax worries took away his hair and the hairbrush. That's why youngsters are running wild today. Dad's run out of weapons.

3 Little Help

MAN: 'I want to buy a pillowcase.'
SALESGIRL: 'What size?'
MAN: 'I'm not sure, but if it'll help, I wear a size 7 hat.'

4 Safe

LITTLE SISTER: 'Bobby, quick, I've dropped my biscuit under the table. Don't let Rover eat it!'
BOBBY: 'Don't worry. I've got my foot on it.'

1 It Takes Time

'Dad, guess what! I've got my first part in a play,' enthused the budding young actor. 'I play the part of a man who's been married for twenty-five years.'

'That's a good start,' replied his Dad. 'Just keep at it and one of these days you'll get a speaking part.'

2 On the Rims

The little girl was telling her teacher about her baby teeth coming out. One tooth was loose and she had already lost three.

She said: 'Soon I'll be running on the rims.'

3 Making Progress

'How many fish have you caught?' asked someone, seeing an old villager fishing on the banks of a stream.

'Well, sir,' replied the old fisherman thoughtfully. 'If I catch this one I'm after, and then two more, I'll have three.'

4 Smart Dad

A young man had become involved in a financial tangle. In a moment of weakness he had lent a friend £500 without getting a receipt. Then the young man found that he needed his money. In desperation he consulted his father.

The father said, 'Oh, that's easy. Write to him and say you need the £1,000 you lent him.'

The young man said, 'You mean £500.'

'I do not,' said the father. 'You say £1,000, and he will immediately write back that he only owes you £500. Then you will have it in writing.'

5 OK

PARK-KEEPER (TO MAN IN POND): 'Hey, you! Can't you see the "No Swimming" notice?'

MAN: 'I'm not swimming, I'm drowning.'

PARK-KEEPER: 'Oh, that's all right then.'

1 He Will

ONLOOKER: 'What a glorious scene! I wish I could take these colours home with me.'
ARTIST: 'You will. You're sitting on my paintbox.'

2 No Details

One woman to another: 'I won't go into all the details. In fact, I've already told you more about it than I heard myself.'

3 Made It Difficult

The man got off the train green in the face. A friend who met him asked him what was wrong.

'Train sickness,' said the traveller. 'I'm always sick when I sit with my back to the engine.'

'Why didn't you ask the person sitting opposite you to change places?' the friend asked.

'I thought of that,' replied the traveller, 'but there wasn't anybody there.'

4 Easy Question

TEACHER: 'Why do swallows fly south in the autumn?'
PUPIL: 'Walking would take too long.'

5 It Pays

Two men were discussing a mutual acquaintance. 'Nice fellow,' said one, 'but have you noticed how he always lets his friends pick up the bill?'

'Yes,' replied the other. 'He has a terrible impediment in his reach.'

6 Salesmanship

'Grandma, were you once a little girl like me?' asked a youngster.

'Why, yes, dear,' answered Grandma, smiling. 'Why do you ask?'

'Then,' continued the little girl, 'I suppose you know how it feels to get an ice cream when you don't expect it.'

1 The Difference

The difference between a psychosis and a neurosis is this. A person with a psychosis thinks that two plus three equals four. A person with a neurosis knows that two plus two equals four, but it bothers him.

2 Music Lover

Little boy, listening to a violinist for the first time: 'Mummy, will we be going home as soon as the man has cut his box in two?'

3 Helpful

Paddy and Sean, panting and pulling on their tandem bicycle, finally reached the top of a long, steep hill.
'Whew!' gasped Paddy. 'What a climb!'
'Sure was!' agreed Sean. 'If I hadn't kept the brake on we'd have gone down backwards.'

4 He Knew

'I'm sorry, sir,' said the boy learning to dive, 'but I couldn't dive from the highest board. It's all of fifteen feet.'
'I know, but you need to conquer your fear,' the instructor answered firmly. 'Supposing you were that high above the water on a sinking ship. What would you do then?'
'Wait for the ship to sink another ten feet.'

5 So It Seems

MOTHER: 'I'm ashamed of you, Susie! Why are you smacking the cat?'
SUSIE: ''Cause he's dirty. He spits on his feet and wipes them on his face.'

6 Be Thankful

'Thankful! What have I to be thankful for?' grumbled the sour-looking man to the sunshine spreader. 'I can't even pay my bills.'
'In that case,' prompted the other readily, 'be thankful that you aren't one of your creditors.'

❝ 1 A Poem about Happy People

The world is so full of a number of things,
Most of them so chaotic,
That those of us who are happy as kings,
Must either be boobs or psychotic.

2 A Poem with a Moral

Mary had a little cold,
But wouldn't stay at home,
And everywhere that Mary went,
The cold was sure to roam.
It wandered into Molly's eyes
And filled them full of tears;
It jumped from there to Bobby's nose,
And thence to Jimmy's ears.
It painted Anna's throat bright red,
And poor Jenny's hurt head;
Emma had a fever, and
A cough put Jack to bed.
The moral of this little tale
Is very quickly said –
Mary could have saved a lot
Of pain, with just one day in bed!

3 Doing Well

'I hear that your son is getting on quite well.'
  'Oh, definitely! Only two years ago he was wearing my old suits.
Now I wear his.'

4 Miracle

After boasting of his prowess, the sportsman took aim at a lone duck
overhead. 'Watch this,' he commanded his listeners.
  He fired, and the bird flew on.
  'My friends,' he said with awe, 'you are now viewing a miracle.
There flies a dead duck!' ❞

1 Add Water

A boat being towed on a trailer had this name: *Instant Fun*, and underneath these words: 'Just add water.'

2 Be Careful

The teacher asked a class discussing North American Indians if anyone could tell her what the leaders of the tribes were called.
'Chiefs,' said a little girl.
'Correct,' said the teacher. 'And what were the women called?'
A little lad answered promptly, 'Mischiefs.'

3 Simply Stated

An economist spoke on the whys and wherefores of budgeting and finance. He spoke for an hour and covered the subject well. Following him, the chairman said:
'Ladies and gentlemen, what our speaker has been telling you is that if your outgoings exceed your income, then your upkeep will be your downfall.'

4 Not a Total Loss

Mountain guide: 'Don't go too near the edge of that precipice – it's dangerous. But if you do fall, remember to look to the left. You'll get a wonderful view.'

5 He Knew

A tourist was visiting New Mexico. While gazing at the dinosaur bones that were all over the place, he met an old Indian who acted as an official guide.
'How old are these bones?' the tourist asked.
'Exactly 100 million and three years old,' the Indian replied.
'How can you be so definite?' the tourist asked.
'Oh,' replied the Indian, 'a geologist told me they were 100 million years old, and that was exactly three years ago.'

❛ 1 Sorry

A man in a restaurant was having trouble cutting his steak. No matter how much pressure he exerted or how much he jabbed at it, he got no results. Finally, he called the waiter. 'I'm afraid you'll have to take this back and bring me another.'

'Sorry, sir,' said the waiter after closely examining the steak. 'I can't take it back. I'm afraid you've bent it.'

2 Did His Best

NEIGHBOUR: 'You have a nice collection of books, but it seems to me you ought to have more shelves.'

SECOND NEIGHBOUR: 'Yes, I know, but no one ever lends me any shelves.'

3 It Helped

'I beg your pardon,' said the man returning to his seat in the theatre, 'but did I step on your toes when I left?'

'You certainly did,' came the reply.

'Good, I'm in the right row.'

4 Hard Luck

UNCLE: 'Hello, my boy. You're not looking very happy. What's the matter?'

SMALL NEPHEW: 'Aunt Rose said I could eat as much ice cream as I wanted – and I can't.'

5 The Smaller Ones

'Willie,' said the teacher, 'can you name the principal river of Egypt?'

'It's the Nile.'

'That's right. Now can you tell me the names of some of the smaller tributaries?'

Willie hesitated, then smiled. 'The juveniles!' **❜**

1 Executive Responsibilities

'My brother's an aquatic engineer in a big restaurant.'
'What's that?'
'He's in charge of the dishwashing there.'

2 Pay No Attention

A motorist was driving in the country when suddenly his car stopped. He got out and was checking the spark plugs when an old horse trotted up the road.

The horse said, 'You'd better check the fuel pump,' and trotted on.

The motorist was so frightened that he ran to the nearest farmhouse and told the farmer what had happened.

'Was it an old horse with a flopping ear?' the farmer asked.

'Yes! Yes!' cried the frightened man.

'Well, don't pay any attention to him,' replied the farmer. 'He doesn't know much about cars.'

3 Not Easy

An elderly lady zoomed past a police car which was cruising along at a nominal speed. The driver chased her, and when he had brought her to a stop he asked for her driving licence.

The woman looked at him sharply. 'Young man,' she said, 'how can I be expected to show you my driving licence when you people keep taking it away?'

'

1 Very Bright

A golf pro, employed by a club to give lessons, was approached by two smarties. 'Do you want to learn to play golf?' the pro asked them.

'Not me,' said one, 'it's Bill here. He wants to learn. I learned yesterday.'

2 Helpful

NEIGHBOUR: 'You say your son gets on your nerves? Why not buy him a bicycle?'
DAD: 'Do you think that would improve his behaviour?'
NEIGHBOUR: 'No, but it would spread it over a wider area!'

3 Not Broke

The young lady told her friend that she was going to marry a rather eccentric millionaire.

'But,' her friend said, 'everyone thinks he's a little bit cracked.'

'He may be cracked,' the young lady said, 'but he certainly isn't broke.'

4 In Real Trouble

The young man rushed in the door exclaiming loudly, 'Darling, I'm ruined. I've lost my job. I'm bankrupt. I haven't a penny.'

His girl said soothingly, 'Don't worry, sweetheart, I'll always love you – even if I never see you again.'

5 Shrewd Observations

The famous detective arrived on the scene.

'Heavens,' he said, 'this is more serious than I thought – the window is broken on both sides.'

6 When We Know We Know

We used to think we knew we knew,
But now we must confess,
The more we know we know we know,
We know we know the less.

'

1 That Explains it?

'Why don't you make love to me like that?' she said as she nudged her husband in the cinema during a love scene.

'Do you realize how much he's paid for that?' he countered.

2 Real Handicap

I cannot sing the old songs
That memories gently bring.
I cannot sing the old songs –
Because I cannot sing!

3 Thoroughly Satisfied

Worried about what to get his girl for a birthday present, the teenager asked, 'Mum, if you were going to be sixteen tomorrow, what would you want?'

Mother, with a faraway look in her eyes, replied: 'Not another thing, son, not another thing.'

4 Good Question

One little boy to another, as they watched the escalator going down: 'What happens when the basement gets full of steps?'

5 He Had Him There

'Remember, son,' said the father, trying to teach a lesson, 'a job well done need never be done again.'

'What about mowing the lawn?' asked the sceptical boy.

6 Not Intentional

A man was chatting with a business acquaintance at lunch. 'We're a non-profit organization,' he said. 'We didn't mean to be, but we are.'

' 1 Golf

I think that I shall never see
A hazard tougher than a tree –
A tree o'er which my ball must fly
If on the green it is to lie;
A tree whose leafy arms extend
To kill the mashie shot I send;
A tree that stands in silence there,
While angry golfers race and swear.
Niblicks are made for fools like me,
Who cannot even miss a tree!

2 Doing Things

There are many ways of doing things,
A casual glance discloses;
Some folks turn up their sleeves at work,
And some turn up their noses.

3 A Poem on Love

Slippery ice, very thin;
Pretty girl tumbled in.
Saw a boy upon the bank –
Gave a shriek, and then she sank.
Boy on bank heard her shout,
Jumped right in – helped her out.
Now he's hers – very nice:
But she had to break the ice.

4 Fiction

A former sales rep says he enjoys reading history, politics and biography. For fictional material, he just skims through a few old expense claims.

5 How Do You Rate?

New executive's slogan: 'If you don't have ulcers, you're not carrying your share of the load.' **'**

1 Wanted to Know Them

A mild little man walked into an income tax inspector's office, sat down and beamed at everyone.

'What can we do for you?' the inspector asked.

'Nothing, thank you,' replied the little man. 'I just wanted to meet the people I'm working for.'

2 Limerick with a New Idea

A lady who lived in East Sheen
Was notoriously stingy and mean.
'If a sandwich,' she said,
'Had but one piece of bread,
There'd be no need for meat in between.'

3 Pretty Bad Story

'What time is it by your watch?'
'Quarter to.'
'Quarter to what?'
'I don't know – times got so bad I had to lay off one of the hands.'

4 He Was Caught

'I got a ticket last Friday because I was driving too slowly.'
'A ticket because you were driving too slowly?'
'Yes. The police caught me.'

5 School Exams Are Funny

How about some of these for exam answers?

William Tell invented the telephone.

In mathematics, Persia gave us the dismal system.

A circle is a round line with no kinks in it, joined up so as not to show where it began.

To keep milk from turning sour, keep it in the cow.

Universal suffrage was when the whole universe was made to suffer.

Savages are people who can't know what wrong is until missionaries show them.

❨ 1 Strategy

A woman turned sweetly to the woman near her as a seat on the crowded bus became available. 'You sit down,' she said. 'You're older than I am.'

The other glared. 'Indeed I am not older than you! Sit down yourself!' she expostulated.

The first lady sat down, smiling comfortably to herself. Several stops later she leaned towards a fellow passenger and confided quietly: 'That remark gets me a seat every time.'

2 Hold It

A doctor and a lawyer were in a bitter dispute. The doctor said, 'A little bird told me what kind of a lawyer you are − "cheep, cheep".'

To which the lawyer retorted, 'Well, a little duck told me what kind of a doctor you are.'

❩

1 Be Careful

A witty driver was speeding through traffic. He soon found himself stopped by an officer of the law. 'Look here,' the policeman growled. 'Where's the fire?'

'What are you worrying about?' the speeder countered. 'You're not a fireman!'

2 Particular

The car stalled at the corner, and the traffic light changed red, yellow, green; red, yellow, green; etc. The polite policeman stepped up beside the driver and asked: 'What's the matter? Don't we have any colours you like?'

3 Less Than Nothing

Many a man in these days has a deficit, and very often he does not know that he has it. A deficit is a very peculiar thing to have. It's what you've got when you haven't as much as you had when you had nothing.

4 History!

AMERICAN BOY (AD 3000): 'What was the origin of the Fourth of July celebration?'

TEACHER: 'Its origin is buried in antiquity. One authority is of the opinion that it was on 4 July that Noah landed with his *Mayflower*, and his sons – Shem, Ham, and Japheth – set off fireworks in honour of the event, the fireworks being provided by Solomon, Queen Elizabeth and the Boston Tea Party. Another authority holds that the festival is purely a civic one, dating from the time St Patrick drove the snakes out of New York.'

5 Absolutely Necessary

A small boy at the zoo asked why the giraffe had such a long neck. 'Well, you see,' said the keeper gravely, 'the giraffe's head is so far removed from his body that a long neck is absolutely necessary.'

❛ 1 Learned Nothin'

Little Tommy had spent his first day at school. Mother was anxious to know how he had got on. 'What did you learn, dear?' she asked.

'Didn't learn nothin',' came the reply.

'Well, then, what did you do?'

'Didn't do nothin'. A woman wanted to know how to spell "dog", an' I told 'er, that's all.'

2 It's OK

'Son, you're always at the bottom of the class.'

'That's all right, Dad, they teach the same things at both ends.'

3 Not Worried

Johnny, who was ill, refused to take his medicine. His mother was in despair.

'You might die,' she said.

'Cheer up,' said Johnny. 'Daddy will be home soon and he'll make me take it.'

4 Bright Lad

TEACHER: 'Who can use the word "income" in a sentence?'

BOY: 'I opened the door and income my cat.'

5 Radio Announcement Blunders

'Go to Smith's shoe shop. There you can be fitted by expert salespeople in all widths and sizes.'

'Anyone who listens to me has had occasion to use aspirin.'

'Small children with families admitted free.'

'It is best to bake a custard standing in a pan of water.' ❜

1 Don't Be a Goop

The Goops they lick their fingers,
And the Goops they lick their knives;
 They spill their broth
 On the tablecloth
And they lead untidy lives.

        Gellet Burgess

2 In Detail

'What will you have with your perm?' asked the stylist in the hairdresser's.

'The inside story of the Smiths' divorce,' replied Mrs McGossip.

3 An Old One

'How will you have your beard trimmed?' the barber asked.

'In silence,' replied the general.

4 More Nonsense

There was a young lady named Bright,
Who could travel much faster than light.
She started one day
In a relative way,
And came back the previous night.

6 Easy to Find

The department store engaged an efficiency expert whose obsession was to move the departments to different parts of the store every day. One day a section would be on the top floor, the next it would be in the basement, and on the third it would be placed where the restaurant had been.

After three weeks of this, an elderly woman approached a harassed assistant and asked him if he could tell her where the linen department was.

'No, madam,' he said wearily, 'but if you'll stand here for a few minutes, I'm sure you'll see it go by.'

1 Don't Stop

'With a car like that, my advice is to keep it moving,' instructed the mechanic.

'Why?' asked the owner.

'If you ever stop, the police will think it's an accident.'

2 He Will Know

ROONEY: Who is your wife going to vote for?'

LOONEY: 'Whoever I vote for.'

ROONEY: 'Who are you going to vote for?'

LOONEY: 'She hasn't decided yet.'

3 Also a Computer

In these times, when a man says the world owes him a living, he includes in that a car, colour television and video.

4 A Famous Limerick

A fly and a flea in a flue
Were imprisoned, so what could they do?
Said the fly, 'Let us flee!'
'Let us fly!' said the flea,
So they flew through a flaw in the flue.

5 Another Limerick

There was a young fellow named Fisher,
Who was fishing for fish in a fissure,
When a cod, with a grin,
Pulled the fisherman in;
Now they're fishing the fissure for Fisher.

6 Something's Wrong

A teenager was discussing her end of term report. 'No wonder Jean always does well in French,' she observed. 'Her father and mother speak French at the table.'

'If that's the case,' her boyfriend said, 'I ought to be top in geometry. My parents talk in circles!'

1 The New Model

When people's cars get old and worn,
And then begin to toddle,
They go somewhere and trade them in,
And get the latest model.
Now, I have very often thought
That when my joints get achy,
And when my hair has all turned grey,
And knees are rather shaky;
And when the onward march of time
Has left me rather feeble,
How nice 'twould be to find a firm
That deals in worn-out people.
And when my form is bent with age,
And gets to looking shoddy,
How nice 'twould be to trade it in,
And get a brand new model!

2 Strange

TEACHER: 'What is the meaning of "fat chance"?'
PUPIL: 'It means you have a slim chance.'

3 Farm Life

A government 'expert' conducting an inspection asked an elderly farmer what time he got up to go to work.

'Young man,' came the reply, 'I don't have to go to work. I wake up in the morning surrounded by it.'

1 Where Else

A shopper reported that someone had taken £30 worth of groceries from her car. 'Did you have them inside the car or in the boot?' the policeman asked.

'No, of course not. I had them in the glove compartment.'

2 Simpler

A wit once said, 'I write down everything I want to remember. That way, instead of spending a lot of time trying to remember what it is I wrote down, I spend the time looking for the paper I wrote it down on.'

3 They Sound That Way

The music publisher was talking about a new song to his promotion manager: 'I've never heard such corny lyrics, such simpering sentimentality, such repetitious, uninspired melody. I'm sure we've got a big hit on our hands.'

4 Modern

The modern young mother was reading a bedtime story to her youngest: 'Then Baby Bear said, "And somebody's been watching my little seven-inch TV set – and didn't even turn it off!"'

5 It Wasn't Easy

'So, your son now drives a car. How long did it take him to learn?'
'About two-and-a-half cars,' replied the father sadly.

6 Hire Her

An employer, interviewing a woman for a job, read her application and said, 'I see your birthday is 12 April. What year?'
Her simple reply was, 'Every year.'

7 Next Question

TEACHER: 'Ginny, can you give me a definition of a volcano?'
GINNY: 'A volcano is a mountain with the hiccups.'

‘ 1 It's Easy

'There's one thing I don't understand,' the passenger said to the pilot on the night flight. 'How do you fly in the dark?'

'Well,' answered the pilot, 'there's a light on the left wing, a light on the right wing, and a light on the tail. All I have to do is keep the plane between the lights.'

2 A New Explanation

The owner of a service station was complaining to an employee about his habitual tardiness. 'It's funny,' he said, 'you're always late and you live right across the street. Now Steve Smith, who lives two miles away, is always on time.'

'There's nothing funny about it,' said the man. 'If Steve is late in the morning, he can hurry, but if I'm late, I'm here.'

3 Naturally

Two health food devotees were discussing food preferences.

'I never eat any food with additives or preservatives and I avoid fruit and vegetables that have been sprayed. I don't eat meat or poultry that has been fattened on chemical feed,' said the first one.

'How do you feel?' asked his friend.

'Hungry!'

4 Don't Try to Be Cute

CAFÉ PATRON: 'Why do you serve your customers instant coffee?'
OWNER: 'So they won't have grounds for complaint.'

5 Life

Each man spoils the one he loves,
And gratifies her wishes –
The rich man showers her with gifts,
While the poor man does the dishes!

❛ 1 Overtime

The personnel manager was interviewing a man for a job. 'How long did you work in the other place?'

'Sixty-five years.'

'Sixty-five years?' exclaimed the manager. 'How old are you?'

'I'm forty.'

'Tell me, how could you work sixty-five years when you're only forty years old?'

'Overtime.'

2 Only One

'Did anyone in your family ever make a brilliant marriage?'

'Only my wife.'

3 It Seems That Way

It is unfortunate that so many people seek something for nothing. It is even more unfortunate when they get it.

4 Seems Correct

When asked to describe steel wool, a young student in an engineering class said he thought it was the fleece of a hydraulic ram.

5 Of Course

The pupil was asked to paraphrase the sentence: 'He was bent on seeing her.'

He wrote: 'The sight of her doubled him up.'

6 Two Against Many

Stepping out on stage between acts at the first production of one of his plays, George Bernard Shaw said to the audience, 'What do you think of it?'

This startled everybody for a few moments, but presently a voice in the stalls cried, 'Rotten!' ❜

'Shaw made a bow and melted the house with one of his Irish smiles. 'My friend,' he said, shrugging his shoulders and indicating the audience in front, 'I quite agree with you, but what are two against so many?'

1 Expansion

The couple told their seven-year-old that they had to move because another baby was coming.

'That won't work,' frowned the youngster. 'He'll just follow us.'

2 Hard Choice

More than any other time in history, mankind faces a crossroads. One path leads to despair and utter hopelessness. The other to total extinction. Let us pray we have the wisdom to choose correctly.

Woody Allen

3 Football Is Different

A husband came home from work and found his wife sobbing in front of the television set. 'How in the world can you get worked up over the troubles of people in those soap operas day after day?' he asked.

'I suppose it's the same as your shouting and getting excited when you see men you don't even know grab a little ball and chase up and down a field with it.'

4 Her View

A husband and wife were playing chess. 'This reminds me of when we were dating,' the wife said.

'We never played chess in those days, Gladys,' the husband said.

'No, but even then it took you two hours to make a move.'

5 One Viewpoint

A patient in hospital woke up after an operation and discovered that his room was dark because the curtains were drawn. The nurse, noticing his confusion, said, 'There was a big fire across the street and we didn't want you to think the operation had failed.''

❛ 1 Simple Question

A man at a party approached a psychiatrist and said, 'Doctor, I understand that you can tell whether a person is intelligent or not by asking some very simple questions. Is that true?'

'Yes,' the doctor said. 'For example, Captain Cook made three voyages around the world and died on one of them. Which one?'

'Ah, doc,' the man said. 'You know I'm no good at history.'

2 After-Dinner Speaker

The banquet had been served and the final cup of coffee poured. The waiters had left the dining room. The noise level was high as the guests joked with each other. Everyone was having a good time.

The chairman whispered to the guest speaker, 'Everybody is enjoying the evening. Do you think I should let them have a few more moments of fun, or would you like me to introduce you now?'

3 Second Thought

The saleswoman watched as a teenager twirled in front of the mirror. 'I adore this dress!' bubbled the girl. 'It's absolutely perfect! I'll take it!'

Then the young shopper paused thoughtfully. 'But in case my mother likes it, can I bring it back?'

❜

1 Being Sure

A small town is one where everyone knows all the news before the paper comes out but merely takes the paper to see whether or not the editor got the stories according to the way they heard them.

2 Real Competition

An American visitor was perturbed because his stories of the wonders of his country made little impression on his English friends. He could not seem to bring home to them the gigantic size of his state, or, for that matter, the superiority of American transport systems. 'You know,' he said at last, 'you can get into a train in the state of Texas at dawn and twenty-four hours later you'll still be in Texas.'

'Ah, yes,' one of his friends politely murmured, 'British Rail run some pretty slow trains too.'

3 Longevity

Several elderly church goers were being asked what they attributed their longevity to. 'And why do you think God has permitted you to reach the age of 98?' one wealthy lady was asked.

Without hesitation she answered, 'I think He is testing the patience of my relatives.'

4 True

One thing is certain and the rest is lies,
Smart guys don't wear loud bow ties.

5 In Writing

Little Johnny was bragging about how fast his father's car could go: '125 miles per hour, and Dad has it in writing from the police.'

6 Faults

Think of your own faults the first part of the night when you are awake and of the faults of others the latter part of the night when you are asleep.

' 1 He Agreed

The young man asked his father for £10 to take his girlfriend to a school dance.

'Here's the £10,' his father said. 'But for goodness' sake, make it go as far as you can.'

And his son's quick reply was, 'Dad, I'll make that £10 go so far you'll never see it again.'

2 Did You Sign It?

One little boy couldn't seem to learn. One day the teacher asked him who had signed Magna Carta. The boy said he didn't know. For over a week the teacher asked him the same question each day, and still he couldn't come up with the right answer.

Finally she called the boy's parents in. 'I don't know if your son can't or won't tell me who signed Magna Carta,' she said with concern.

'Come over here and sit down, Tommy,' the father said. 'Now, I don't want you to lie to me. If you signed the crazy thing, admit it and let's get out of here.'

3 Real Flattery

'To what do you owe your extraordinary success?' the company's top house-to-house salesman was asked.

'To the first four words I say when a woman opens the door,' he replied. 'They go like this: "Is your mother in?"'

4 He Isn't Reasonable

Two secretaries were chatting over lunch. 'How do you like your new boss?' the first asked.

'He's all right, I suppose,' said her friend. 'But he's very prejudiced.'

'You mean about women's lib and all that?' the first secretary asked.

'Oh, no, nothing like that,' her friend said. 'He just thinks there's only one way to spell a word.' **'**

❛ 1 He Got Along Well

The five-year-old boy was terribly spoilt. His grandparents knew it. The neighbours knew it. But his mother doted on him. He hardly left her side. And when he wanted anything, he whined, cried or threw a tantrum. Then came his first day at school.

At the end of the day his mother met him. 'Did you get along all right? Did you cry?' she asked.

'Cry?' he asked. 'No, I didn't cry, but the teacher did.'

2 Speechless

How much time is wasted in meaningless chitchat! When the telephone was invented, someone told the famous American writer Henry Thoreau that the people in Massachusetts could talk to the people in Texas. Thoreau wisely questioned, 'But suppose the people in Massachusetts have nothing to say to the people in Texas?'

3 Tongue Twister

The world's worst tongue twister is supposedly: 'The sixth sick sheik's sixth sheep's sick.' Don't trip over your tongue!

4 He Objected

The candidate began his speech by welcoming the audience and saying he was very happy to have such a dense crowd. With that a man rose from his seat and began to leave, shouting, 'Don't be so offensive! We're not all dense.'

5 Silence

The man was sitting in the gutter listening to the kerb. A policeman walked over and asked what he was doing. The man said, 'Come on down here and listen.'

The policeman got on his hands and knees and then got right back up and said, 'I can't hear anything!'

'That's the way it's been all day,' replied the man. ❜

1 Let Him Eat Cake

A tramp asking for a hand-out at a farmhouse door said, 'Lady, can you spare some cake?'

'I'm afraid not,' she said. 'Wouldn't some bread and butter do?'

'As a rule it would,' answered the tramp, 'but you see, today's my birthday!'

2 What Did You Say?

TEACHER: 'Can you hear me?'
BOY: 'No, sir.'
TEACHER: 'If you can't hear me, how can you answer "No"?'

3 It's True

The shoe salesman had shown the woman more than twenty pairs of shoes before she finally settled on the first pair she had tried on. As she was leaving, he said to her, 'Thank you for coming. I wish I had a dozen customers like you.'

One of the other assistants heard him, and when the customer had gone he said, 'You told her you wished you had a dozen customers like her. Why did you say that to such an overbearing and hard-to-please person?'

'Because it's true,' the salesman said. 'I have a hundred like her and I wish I had only a dozen.'

4 No Change

While shopping, two young ladies ran into each other for the first time in weeks. 'It's good to see you,' the first one said. 'I haven't seen you since your engagement party. Have you set the date for the wedding?'

'The wedding is off,' her friend said.

'What happened?' the first woman asked.

'Nothing special,' her friend said. 'I found that my love for him became weaker and weaker and finally disappeared.'

'That's too bad,' the first one said. 'Did you return his ring?'

'Oh, no,' her friend said. 'My love for the ring is as strong as ever.'

1 Advice

The frantic father called the doctor late at night. 'Please hurry,' he said. 'My twelve-year-old boy just swallowed a small ballpoint pen.'

'I'll be there in about twenty minutes,' the doctor said.

'What should I do until you get here?' the man wanted to know.

'Use a pencil,' the doctor said.

2 Is That Right?

SIX-YEAR-OLD: 'Why must I still do arithmetic now that I'm in the second form?'

DADDY: 'Do you always get your sums right?'

SIX-YEAR-OLD (CONFIDENTLY): 'Yes. Today we did five and I got four right and two wrong.'

3 Too Late

In a school essay on parents, a little girl wrote: 'We get our parents when they are so old it is very hard to change their habits.'

4 Common Knowledge

A hotel guest and her six-year-old son were at the desk and the receptionist remarked to the mother: 'You have a cute little boy there.'

Immediately the dignified little boy said, coldly: 'She knows.'

5 His Opinion

When someone asked Groucho Marx to join a club, he said: 'You don't think I'd join any club that would have me for a member, do you?'

6 He Does That Now

'Now,' said the golf professional, 'suppose you just go through the motions without hitting the ball.'

'But,' protested the pupil, 'that's just the difficulty I'm trying to overcome.'

' **1 The Dignity of Labour**

Labour rises honest sweat;
Leisure puts you into debt.
Labour gives you rye and wheat;
Leisure gives you naught to eat.
Labour makes you bed at eight;
Leisure lets you stay up late.
Labour makes you swell with pride;
Leisure makes you shrink inside.
Labour keeps you fit and prime,
But give me leisure every time.

Robert Bersohn

2 Stairs

Here's to the man who invented stairs
And taught our feet to soar!
He was the first who ever burst
Into a second floor.

The world would be downstairs today
Had he not found the key;
So let his name go down to fame,
Whatever it may be.

Oliver Herford

3 That Would Help

WIFE TO SEASICK HUSBAND: 'Do you want me to ask the steward to
  bring some dinner?'
HUSBAND: 'No, but I wish you'd have him take it on deck and throw
  it over the rail for me.'

,

❝ 1 Eat Here

A sign outside the cafeteria at the University of Colorado proclaims: 'Shoes are required to eat in the cafeteria.' Underneath, an undergraduate wrote: 'Socks may eat wherever they feel like.'

2 Two Prizes

CHERYL: 'When did you get that pretty silver medal?'
CAROL: 'I won it in a singing contest.'
CHERYL: 'And how about that even prettier gold one?'
CAROL: 'I got that one at the same contest. They gave it to me for stopping!'

3 An Exception

A minister received this letter:
    'Dear Reverend: I know that God loves everybody, but he never met my sister.
    'Yours truly, Arnold (age 8).'

4 Try Again

A young man got a job at a bank. The first day at work the chief cashier handed him a packet of crisp new notes. 'Here,' he said, 'count these and see if there are 100.'
    The new employee started counting. He got up to 58, stopped counting and dropped the package into the cash drawer. 'No sense counting any further,' he commented to the cashier. 'If it's OK so far, it's probably right all the way.'

5 Would be Helpful

The eight-year-old wanted to decorate his room, so he wrote to his local football club and asked for 'stickers, brochures, and pennance'. A few days later he received a package with this letter, 'We are sending you the brochures and stickers but would suggest that for pennance you spend an hour a day with the Oxford Dictionary.' ❞

69

‘ 1 Obedient

The father of five children won a toy at a raffle. He called the family together to ask which one of them should receive the present.

'Who is the most obedient?' he asked. 'Who never answers Mummy back? Who does everything she says without argument?'

Five small voices answered his questions in unison: 'You play with it, Daddy!'

2 The Same

TEACHER: 'This story on "A Dog" is exactly the same as the composition your brother wrote.'

LITTLE GIRL: 'Yes. We described the same dog.'

3 He Needed Help

At the end of the day, one of the bank clerks was closing the door when he noticed a customer outside with bundles in his arms and a perplexed look on his face, staring at the night safe. The clerk approached him and asked if he could help.

The man turned to him and replied excitedly: 'I hope so. My wife is going to be angry!'

'What happened?'

'I dropped the wrong package in.'

'What was in it?'

'Pork chops.'

4 She Wanted to Be Right

She applied for a job as a typist and they gave her a spelling test.

'How do you spell Mississippi?' she was asked.

'The river or the state?'

5 Unintelligible

'What is your new baby brother's name?' the teacher asked the little girl.

'I don't know,' she said. 'I can't understand a word he says.' **’**

70

1 Trying to Learn

PUPIL: 'What's a green worm, teacher?'
TEACHER: 'I don't know. What is it?'
PUPIL: 'I don't know either – but there's one on your collar.'

2 Reminded Him of Teacher

PUPIL: 'I remember the story about the donkey that you told us last
  year.'
TEACHER: 'It was funny, wasn't it?'
PUPIL: 'Very funny. I never see a donkey without thinking of you.'

3 The Source

MRS SMITH: 'Whenever I'm down in the dumps, I get myself a new
  hat.'
MRS JONES: 'I've often wondered where you got them.'

4 Now or Never

Oliver Wendell Holmes, the late and great US Supreme Court
justice, was once asked why he had taken up the difficult study of
Greek at the age of ninety-four.

'Why, my good man, it's now or never.'

5 Too Busy with Breakfast

TEENAGE BROTHER: 'I thought I told you not to tell Mum and Dad
  what time I got home last night.'
SISTER: 'I didn't. I just said I was too busy getting my breakfast to
  look at the clock.'

6 Free TV

A man stopped at a motel and asked for a room.

'Do you want a £25 room or a £30 room?' asked the manager. 'The
£30 room comes with a free television.'

❛ 1 On His Own

We telephoned an executive who's with one of the larger industrial enterprises. 'He's out to lunch,' his secretary confided, 'but he won't be gone long – nobody took him.'

2 Is That Possible

A GUIDE, ESCORTING A TOUR GROUP THROUGH THE BRITISH MUSEUM: 'The Egyptian mummy in front of you is over 5,000 years old. It's possible that Moses saw it.'

TOURIST: 'Moses saw it? When was Moses ever in London?'

❜

1 Careful

Running into her ex-boyfriend at a party, a woman decided to snub him. 'So sorry,' she murmured when the hostess introduced him, 'but I didn't get your name.'

'I know you didn't,' said he, unabashed, 'but you certainly tried.'

2 Puzzling

A man tried to telephone a friend about two o'clock in the morning but dialled a wrong number. He said he was sorry and dialled again. The same sleepy voice answered.

'I'm sorry,' the man said, 'I was very careful when I dialled. I don't understand how I keep getting you.'

'I don't understand it, either,' the sleepy voice said. 'I don't even have a telephone.'

3 Better Then

The army lieutenant received a complaint about the bread his men were getting.

'Soldiers should not make a fuss about trivialities, my man,' he said. 'If the troops had had that bread in the trenches, they would have eaten it with delight.'

'Yes, sir,' said the corporal, 'but it was fresh then.'

4 No Disclosure

The businessperson who hates being asked 'Who's calling?' when making a telephone call also dislikes having calls answered with a phone number. But everything fell into place one morning:

'8412,' answered the secretary, who was guarding her supply of good morning greetings.

'May I speak to Mr Abernathy?' asked the caller, slightly annoyed.

'May I tell him who's calling?' enquired the secretary.

'5774,' came the remarkably controlled reply.

' 1 That's Extra

HUSBAND: 'See, I fixed that little electrical problem that would have cost us a big bill if you had called an electrician.'
WIFE: 'But how come the lights go off when I turn on the hot water tap?'

2 A New Explorer

A young schoolboy faced an oral exam in history and knew that he would be asked, 'Who discovered America?' He knew that it was Christopher Columbus but was afraid he might forget as he stood up in class, so he pinned the answer inside his blazer.

The next morning the teacher called his name, and as he stood up she asked the dreaded question. The boy opened the wrong side of his blazer, peeped in and answered proudly: 'St Michael'.

3 Pretend

The little girl asked, 'Daddy, why is Mummy singing.'
'To get the baby to go to sleep.'
'Will she stop when the baby goes to sleep?'
'Yes dear.'
'Then I wonder,' said the little girl, 'why the baby doesn't just pretend to be asleep.'

4 Only Licks Them

The customer in the bakery shop asked the little girl who was helping if she ever ate the cakes. 'Oh, no,' replied the child. 'That would be stealing. I just lick them!'

5 Usually True

We have a nice address book,
A book that's sure to give
The names and the addresses
Where people used to live.

‘

1 Overdoing It

A feminist boarded a crowded tube train and a gentleman who had been sitting down stood up. As he started to rise, she forced him back into his seat. He tried again with the same result. At his third try, he said very firmly, 'Miss, you simply must let me get up. I'm already four stops beyond my station.'

2 All Wrong

Asked how he'd enjoyed his recent fishing trip with his dad, the youngster confessed that it was a disaster.

'I did absolutely everything wrong,' he moaned. 'I talked too loud, I used the wrong bait, I reeled in too soon – and I caught more than he did.'

3 A Second Language

A mother mouse and her baby were scampering across a floor when they heard a noise. They hoped it was a human being, but it turned out to be the family cat.

Upon seeing the mice, the cat gave chase. Mother mouse felt a swipe and a claw.

She turned in her tracks and called out in her loudest voice, 'Bow-wow!' The cat ran off.

Gathering her baby to her and catching her breath, the mother mouse explained, 'Now you see the importance of a second language.'

4 His Plan

'Well, young man,' his girlfriend's father said, 'you've asked permission to marry my daughter. Do you think you can support a family?'

'No sir, I can't,' he said. 'I was only planning to support your daughter. The rest of you will have to get along the best you can.' ’

1 Passing Judgment

Arriving for a visit, the woman asked her small granddaughter, 'Tracey, how do you like your new baby brother?'

'Oh, he's all right,' the child shrugged. 'But there were a lot of things we needed more.'

2 Suicidal

A new patient confided to the psyciatrist, 'I'd better tell you before we begin – I suffer from marked suicidal tendencies.'

'Very interesting,' said the psychiatrist. 'Under the circumstances then, I'm quite sure you wouldn't mind paying the bill in advance.'

3 Secret to Success

Rise early.
Work late.
Strike oil!

4 Father Taught Him

TEACHER: 'What is capital punishment?'
PUPIL (WHOSE FATHER IS A BUSINESSMAN): 'It's when the government sets up business in competition with you and then takes all your profits and tax to make up its loss.'

5 Right Place

CUSTOMER: 'Waiter, I'm so hungry I could eat a horse.'
WAITER: 'You came to the right place, sir.'

6 He Knew How Now

'Don't worry,' the nurse said to the woman she was preparing for the operating theatre. 'The surgeon told me this morning that he watched an operation just like this on television last night.'

1 When You Know

You know you are getting old when:
You turn out the lights for economic rather than romantic reasons.
Your knees buckle and your belt won't.
A fortune teller offers to read your face rather than the lines in your hand.
You have too much room in the house and not enough in the medicine cabinet.

2 Making Sure

One of those high-powered, self-important company executives had to go into hospital. Barking orders left and right, he had his own way until he reached the desk of a small, mild-mannered lady. She typed the man's name on a slip of paper, stuck the paper into a plastic bracelet and then snapped it on the man's wrist before he could react.
'What's this for?' demanded Mr Big.
'That,' replied the woman, 'is so we won't give you to the wrong mother when you're ready to leave.'

3 No Improvement

When the white man discovered America, the Indians were running it – no taxes or debt, no bureaucrats, no income tax forms. The white man thought he could improve on a system like that.

4 Almost

A child's letter read, 'Dear Aunt Sarah: The present you sent for Christmas was almost as good as the one I really wanted!'

5 From a Fly's Viewpoint

Two flies were resting and chatting on the ceiling. 'Humans are so silly,' the first fly said. 'They spend all this money building a beautiful ceiling like this and then walk on the floor!'

' 1 Couldn't Be

'How much is 9 eggs plus 7 eggs?' asked the teacher.
  Tommy's hand shot up. 'I think it's 18,' he said.
'No! Stop guessing, Tommy.'
'Then it's 17,' he said.
'No, Tommy. It's 16!'
'That can't be,' the little boy argued. 'You said 8 and 8 are 16.'

2 Frank

The vicar had been invited for dinner. After the meal, he said, 'That was a wonderful meal. It isn't often that I eat such a dinner as we just had.'
  'Neither do we,' the little boy next to him said honestly.

3 The Speed of Light

The teacher had just told his class the speed of light. 'So even though the sun is about 93 million miles away,' he concluded, 'its light reaches us in just a little over 8 minutes. Isn't that amazing?'
  'Not really,' one pupil shrugged. 'It's downhill all the way.'

4 Worse

A friend once wrote Mark Twain a letter stating that he was in very bad health and concluding: 'Is there anything worse than having toothache and earache at the same time?'
  The humorist wrote back: 'Yes, rheumatism and St Vitus's dance.'

5 Good to Have Them Home

Orville and Wilbur Wright had tried repeatedly to fly a heavier-than-air craft. Finally one December day, off the sand dunes of Kitty Hawk, Carolina, they did it. It was the greatest news scoop of the century. Elated, they wired their sister Katherine, 'We have actually flown one hundred twenty feet. Will be home for Christmas.' Hastily she ran down the street and shoved the telegram at the editor of the local paper. 'Well, well,' he smiled, 'isn't it nice that they will be home for Christmas.' '

' ## 1 Winston Churchill vs. Nancy Astor

In 1919 Nancy Astor became the first woman ever to be elected to the House of Commons. During a heated exchange with Winston Churchill one day in Parliament, she told him: 'If you were my husband, Winston, I'd poison your coffee!'

'If you were my wife, Nancy,' he replied, 'I'd drink it.'

2 Candour

Thomas Edison hated formal dinners, which seemed stuffy to him. One night at a particularly dull gathering, he decided to sneak away and return to his laboratory.

As he was pacing back and forth near the door, waiting for an opportune moment to escape, a friend came up to him.

'It certainly is a delight to see you, Mr Edison,' he said. 'What are you working on now?'

'My exit,' replied the inventor.

3 Prize Winner

There was a young man of Devizes,
Whose ears were of different sizes;
    The one that was small
    Was of no use at all,
But the other won several prizes.

'

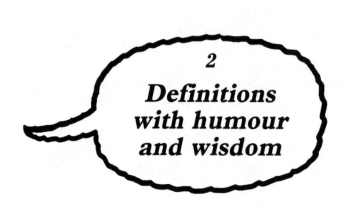

2
Definitions with humour and wisdom

...A...

1 Ability:

The art of getting credit for all the successes that somebody else makes.

2 Abstract art:

A product of the untalented, sold by the unprincipled to the utterly bewildered.   *Al Capp*

3 Accomplice:

One who lacks brains as well as honesty.

4 Actor:

A man who can walk to the side of a stage, peer into the wings filled with dust, other actors, stagehands, old clothes and other claptrap, and say, 'What a lovely view there is from this window.'   *Variety*

' 1 Adolescence:

The awkward age when a child is too old to say something cute and too young to say something sensible.

2 Adolescence:

The period when children are certain they will never be as stupid as their parents.

3 Adolescent:

One who is well informed about anything he doesn't have to study.

4 Adult education:

What goes on in a household containing teenage children.

5 Advertisement:

The most truthful part of a newspaper.   *Thomas Jefferson*

6 Advertising:

The fine art of making you think you have longed all your life for something you never heard of before.

7 Afternoon:

The part of the day spent working out how you wasted the morning.

8 Afterthought:

A tardy sense of prudence that prompts one to try to shut his mouth about the time he has put his foot in it.

9 Alphabet:

A toy for children found in books, blocks, pictures and some soup. '

❛ 1 Ambition:

A poor excuse for not having sense enough to be lazy.

Charlie McCarthy

2 Ambulance:

The shuttle between a speeding car and a wheelchair.

3 America:

A nation that conceives many odd inventions for getting somewhere but can think of nothing to do when it gets there.

Will Rogers

4 Americans:

People with more time-saving devices and less time than any other people in the world. *Thomaston Times (Georgia)*

5 Ancestor worship:

The conviction that your family is better dead than alive.

6 Anger:

Momentary madness. *Horace*

7 Animals:

Creatures that do not grab for more when they have enough.

8 Antique:

An object that has made a round-trip to the attic and back.

9 Antiques:

Furniture that is too old for the poor folks but the right age for the rich. **❜**

' **1 Apartment:**

A place where you try to turn off your radio and discover you've been listening to your neighbour's.

2 Apologise:

To repeat an insult with variations.

3 Appeaser:

One who feeds a crocodile – hoping it will eat him last.
Winston Churchill

4 April 1st:

The day we are reminded of what we are the other 364.
Mark Twain

5 Argument:

Something that gets better when you don't have facts.

6 Arithmetic:

Being able to count up to 20 without taking off your shoes.
Mickey Mouse

7 Arthritis:

Twinges in the hinges.

8 Atheist:

A man who believes himself an accident.   *Francis Thompson*

9 Atheist:

One who prays when he can think of no other way out of his trouble.
Prison Mirror '

'
1 Athlete, amateur:

An athlete who is paid only in cash − not by cheque.

2 Auctioneer:

One who can equally and impartially admire all schools of art.

Oscar Wilde

3 Autobiography:

An unrivalled vehicle for telling the truth about other people.

4 Awe:

Showing respect with your mouth wide open.

'

...B...

1 Baby:

A perfect example of minority rule.   *Milwaukee Journal*

2 Bachelor:

A thing of beauty and a boy forever.   *Helen Rowland*

3 Backbiter:

A mosquito.

4 Bald:

When one has less hair to comb but more face to wash.

5 Barber:

A brilliant conversationalist who cuts hair as a sideline.

6 Bargain:

Usually something that's so reasonable they won't take it back when you find out what's wrong with it.

7 Benefactor:

One who returns part of his loot.

8 Benefactor:

One who makes two smiles grow where one grew before.

9 Benevolence:

The distinguishing characteristic of man.   *Mencius*

1 Bestseller:

The gilded tomb of a mediocre talent.

2 Bigamy:

The only crime on the books where two rites make a wrong.
Bob Hope

3 Birth:

The beginning of death.

4 Birthday:

Anniversary of one's birth, observed only by children.

5 Budget:

A family's attempt to live below its yearnings.

6 Budget:

A plan that tells you what you can afford to spend but doesn't keep you from spending more.

7 Budget:

A schedule for going into debt systematically.

8 Budget:

Telling your money where to go instead of wondering where it went.   *C. E. Hoover*

9 Buffet supper:

Where the hostess doesn't have enough chairs for everybody.

1 Bus conductor:

The person who tells everyone where to get off.

2 Business:

Something which, if you don't have any, you go out of.

3 Business economy:

A reduction in the other fellow's salary.

4 Business forecaster:

A person who is uncertain about the future and hazy about the present.

5 Businessman:

An amateur gardener who does his spring digging with a golf club.

6 Businessman:

The man to whom age brings golf instead of wisdom.

George Bernard Shaw

'   ...C...

1 Candidate:

A person who asks for money from the wealthy and votes from the poor to protect them from each other.

2 Car:

A guided missile.

3 Cauliflower:

A cabbage with a college education.   *Mark Twain*

4 Centenarian:

A person who has lived to be 100 years old. He never smoked or he smoked all his life. He drank whisky for 80 years or he never drank it. He was a vegetarian or he wasn't a vegetarian. Follow these rules carefully and you too can be a centenarian.

5 Chairman or toastmaster:

A person who introduces a person who doesn't need an introduction.

6 Chairman or toastmaster:

A person who introduces someone who is already well known to the audience.

7 Cheerfulness:

The art of concealing your true feelings.

8 Chef:

An interior decorator.

' 1 Chicken:

An egg factory.

2 Christian nation:

One that has churches that too many people stay away from on Sunday.

3 City life:

Millions of people being lonely together.   *Henry David Thoreau*

4 Classic:

A book which people praise and don't read.   *Mark Twain*

5 Combustion:

What takes place when there aren't enough goods in a store to cover the insurance.

6 Commercial:

The warning you get to turn down the television.

7 Conceited person:

One who mistakes a big head for greatness.

8 Conference:

A long coffee break.

9 Conscience:

A still, small voice that tells when you are about to get caught.   **'**

' 1 Contortionist:

The only person who can do what everyone else would like to do –
pat himself on the back.

2 Cookbook:

A volume that is full of stirring passages.

3 Coordinator:

The person who has a desk between expeditors.

4 Corporation:

An ingenious device for obtaining individual profit without
individual responsibility.   *Ambrose Bierce*

5 Country:

A kind of healthy grave.   *Sydney Smith*

6 Country and western superstar:

Someone who gets rich by singing about how wonderful it is to be
poor.

7 Courage:

Ignorance of the facts.

8 Cow:

A machine that makes it possible for people to eat grass.

9 Coward:

One who in a perilous emergency thinks with his legs.

Ambrose Bierce **'**

'

1 Crank:

A person who insists on convincing you instead of letting you convince him.

2 Crochet:

An exercise that gives women something to think about when they are talking.

3 Croquet:

Chess with sweat.

'

'   **...D...**

1 Deficit:

What you have when you don't have as much as if you had nothing.

2 Deluxe:

Mediocre in a big way.

3 Dentist:

A collector of old magazines.

4 Dentist:

A person who runs a filling station.

5 Desk:

A waste basket with drawers.   *Wall Street Journal*

6 Diamond:

A hunk of coal that stuck to its job.

7 Diamond:

A piece of coal that made good under pressure.

8 Diet:

A selection of foods for people who are thick and tired of it.

9 Diplomacy:

Telling your boss he has an open mind instead of telling him he has holes in his head.

10 Diplomacy:

The patriotic art of lying for one's country.   *Ambrose Bierce*   **'**

1 Diplomat:

A rabbit in a silk hat.

2 Diplomat:

One who can yawn with his mouth closed.

3 Discretion:

When you are sure you are right and then ask your wife.

4 Doctor:

A man who has his tonsils, adenoids and appendix.

5 Driver, careful:

The man who has made the last payment on his car.

. . .E. . .

6 Economy:

Spending money without getting any fun out of it.

7 Education:

The transmission of civilization.

8 Efficiency:

Getting someone to do a job you hate.

9 Egg:

A day's work for a hen.

1 Endless:

The time it takes for others to find out how wonderful you are.

2 Englishman:

One who objects when a foreigner curses the institutions he curses.

3 Etc.:

A sign you use in writing to make people believe you know more than you do.

4 Etiquette:

Knowing which finger to put in your mouth when you whistle for the waiter.

5 Executive:

A person who makes a prompt decision and is sometimes right.

6 Executive:

A person who talks golf in the office and business on the golf course.

7 Experience:

What you get while looking for something else.

8 Experience:

We should be careful to get out of an experience only the wisdom that is in it — and stop there; lest we be like the cat that sits down on a hot stove-lid. She will never sit down on a hot stove-lid again — and that is well; but also she will never sit down on a cold one any more.   *Mark Twain*

1 Expert:

One who avoids the small errors as he sweeps to the big mistake.

2 Expert:

A person who knows enough to complicate simple matters.

3 Expert:

Someone who is called in at the last moment to share the blame.

'   **...F...**

1 Fad:

Something that goes in one era and out the other.

2 Failure:

The opportunity to begin again – more wisely.

3 Fanatic:

One who can't change his mind and won't change the subject.
Winston Churchill

4 Flattery:

Often an insult in gift wrapping.

5 Footnote:

Useless information placed where you can skip it.

6 Friend:

A person who listens attentively while you say nothing.

7 Friend:

Someone who doesn't believe the gossip he hears about you even if he knows it's true.

8 Friend:

Someone who knows you well and still likes you.

'

...G...

1 Garage:

An attic on a lower level.

2 Gentility:

What is left over from rich ancestors after the money is gone.

3 Gentleman:

A man who never hurts anyone's feelings unintentionally.

4 Goblet:

A small turkey.

5 Golf:

A game in which purple people pursue white balls over green hills.

6 Gossip:

Something that goes in one ear and over the back fence.

7 Grandparent:

One who knows that spanking is unnecessary.

8 Grapefruit:

Eyewash.

9 Gunpowder:

A substance used to make nations friendly to each other.

' ...H...

1 Headlights:

What the car driver uses to blind oncoming drivers.

2 Helpless:

The feeling you have when your goldfish is sick.

3 Hobby:

Something you get worked up about to keep from going nuts about things in general.

4 Holiday:

A succession of 2s. It consists of 2 weeks, which are 2 short. Afterwards, you are 2 tired 2 return 2 work and 2 broke not 2.

5 Holiday:

Two weeks off, often followed by two off weeks.

6 Honesty:

The greatest handicap you can have in golf.

7 Horse sense:

Something a horse has that keeps him from betting on men.

8 Humility:

The solid foundation of all the virtues. *Confucius*

9 Husband:

A man of few words.

...I...

1 Icicle:
A stiff piece of water.

2 Imagination:
What makes some politicians think they're statesmen.

3 Inflation:
Being broke with a lot of money in your pocket.

4 Inflation:
When one can live as cheaply as two.

5 Inflation:
When you can't have your cake. Dieting is when you can't eat it.

6 Instalment buying:
A way to make the months seem shorter or to make time fly.

...J...

7 Jack:
A thing that lifts a car and also keeps it going.

8 Jewellery:
A woman's best friend.

' 1 Jumble sale:

Where you buy stuff from other people's attics to put in your own.

2 Junk:

Something you throw away two weeks before you need it.

3 Justice:

A decision in your favour.

...K...

4 Kangaroo:

Nature's initial effort to produce a cheerleader.

...L...

5 Life:

A do-it-yourself project.

...M...

6 Man:

The only animal that cooks.

7 Man:

The only animal with brains enough to find a cure for the diseases caused by his own folly. **'**

1 Manners:

Noises you don't make when eating soup.

2 Mealtime:

When the children sit down to continue eating.

3 Middle age:

That period in life when your idea of getting ahead is staying even.

4 Middle age:

When the average person is going to begin saving next month.

5 Middle age:

When you begin to exchange your emotions for symptoms.

6 Middle age:

When you want to see how long your car will last instead of how fast it will go.

7 Middle class:

The people who live in public like the rich do – and in private like the poor do.

8 Money:

The best substitute there is for credit.

9 Money:

Workers earn it, spendthrifts burn it, bankers lend it, women spend it, forgers fake it, taxes take it, people dying leave it, heirs receive it, thrifty people save it, misers crave it, robbers seize it, the rich increase it, gamblers lose it – we could use it.

1 Mystery

How the Joneses do it on that salary.

...N...

2 Naive person:

Anyone who thinks you are interested when you ask how he is.

3 Neighbour:

A person who is out of something.

4 Nero:

A Roman who was careless with candles.

5 Nurses:

Patient people.

...O...

6 Obstinate person:

One who doesn't hold opinions; they hold him.

7 Operation, minor:

One performed on someone else.

8 Optimist:

A fisherman who takes a camera with him when he goes fishing.

1 Optimist:

A person who looks forward to enjoying the scenery on a detour.

2 Optimist:

One who laughs to forget, whereas a pessimist forgets to laugh.

3 Optimist:

Someone who sets aside an afternoon to do Christmas shopping.

4 Optimist:

The person who thinks he will never be a sucker again.

5 Oratory:

The art of making deep sounds from the chest seem like important messages from the brain.

6 Organ:

A large upright bagpipe.

7 Originality:

The art of concealing your source.

...P...

8 Parents:

Hardships of children.

9 Patience:

The companion of wisdom. *St Augustine*

1 Patience:

The quality you admire in the driver behind you but can't stand in the driver in front of you.

2 Patriot:

The person who is sorry he has but one income to give to his country.

3 Peace:

A short period between wars.

4 Pessimist:

A person who is happy when he is wrong.

5 Philosophy:

Common sense in a smart suit.

6 Philosophy:

The system of being unhappy intelligently.

7 Picnic:

An ant's lunch.

8 Plumber:

A person who hangs out under people's sinks.

9 Poise:

The ability to act so that no one suspects how ill at ease you really are.

1 Poise:

The ability to be at ease conspicuously.

2 Poise:

The ability to be ill at ease naturally.

3 Politician:

A Goon with the wind.   *Bob Hope*

4 Possibly:

'No' or 'yes' in three syllables.

5 Praise:

The sweetest of all sounds.

6 Prejudice:

A great time-saver that enables one to form opinions without bothering to get the facts.

7 Primitive artist:

An amateur whose work sells.   *Grandma Moses*

8 Procrastination:

The greatest time-saver of all.

9 Procrastinator:

One who puts off until tomorrow the things he has already put off until today.

10 Proof of purchase:

An empty wallet.

1 Prosperity:

Something created by hard-working citizens for politicians to boast about.

2 Prosperity:

Something you feel, fold and sent to the Inland Revenue.

3 Psychiatrist:

Someone who, when a pretty woman enters the room, watches everyone else.

...R...

4 Rare volume:

A borrowed book that comes back.

5 Reformer:

Someone who wants his conscience to be your guide.

6 Reindeer:

Horses with hatracks.

7 Relative, distant:

A relative who owes you money.

8 Relative, distant:

One who can be very distant – especially when he has lots of money.

1 Relativity:

When a man sits with a pretty girl for an hour, it seems like a minute. But let him sit on a hot stove for a minute – and it's longer than any hour. That's relativity.   *Albert Einstein*

2 Resort:

A place where people go for sunshine and fresh air and then sit indoors and watch TV all day.

3 Resort:

A town where the inhabitants live on your holiday money until next summer.

4 Retraction:

To make one take back a statement. For example: A newspaper headline said, 'Half of City Council Are Crooks.' The City Council demanded a retraction. The next day the headline said, 'Half the City Council Are Not Crooks.'

5 Ringleader:

The first in a large family to take a bath on Saturday night.

6 Road hog:

A car driver who meets you more than halfway.

7 Rock:

The kind of music that, no matter what notes you play, always sounds wrong.

8 Runner, marathon:

A person who is happy to be over the hill.

(1 Rush hour:

When you travel the shortest distance in the longest time.

...S...

2 Scotsman:

The only golfer who wouldn't knock a golf ball out of sight.

3 Security:

When I'm very much in love with somebody extraordinary who loves me back.   *Shelley Winters*

4 Self-control:

The ability to carry a credit card and not abuse it.

5 Silence:

Having nothing to say and saying it.

6 Small town:

A place where everybody knows whose cheque is good.

7 Small town:

The place where one always looks around to see if anyone is related to the fellow about whom he is about to make an unkind remark.

8 Smart fellow:

A person who says what he thinks, provided he agrees with us.

9 Statesman:

A politician away from home.   **)**

'

1 Statesmanship:

The art of changing a nation from what it is to what it ought to be.

2 Statistics:

This thing called statistics was the worst thing that was invented; it's the curse of the world. We wouldn't know how bad the others were doing if we didn't have statistics.   *Will Rogers*

3 Success:

A country shopkeeper retired with a fortune of £100,000. That was success. His ability to retire with £100,000, after forty years, was due to hard work, strict attention to duty, absolute honesty, economical living and the recent death of his uncle, who left him £98,500.

4 Successful wife's motto:

If at first you don't succeed, cry, cry again.

'

'

. . . T . . .

1 Tact:

The art of making a point without making an enemy.

2 Tailor:

A person who does sew-sew work.

3 Tax:

A fine for doing all right. A fine is a tax for doing wrong.

4 Teacher, best:

The one who makes you want to learn.

'

1 Teenager:

One who is old enough to know everything.

2 Television:

A device that permits people who haven't anything to do to watch people who can't do anything.

3 Television:

Chewing gum for the eyes.   *Frank Lloyd Wright*

4 Thrift:

A wonderful virtue – especially in an ancestor.

5 Thrift:

Common sense applied to spending.   *Theodore Roosevelt*

6 Tomorrow:

The day you are going to clean out the garage.

7 Toot ensemble:

Two hundred cars waiting for a green light at a busy junction on a Sunday afternoon.

8 Tragedy:

A bride without a can opener.

9 Triumph:

'Umph' added to 'try'.

'

1 Vacuum cleaner:

A broom with a stomach.

2 Vote:

When you have a chance to choose the lesser of evils.

3 War:

A passion play performed by idiots.

4 Wind:

Weather on the go.

5 Woman, intelligent:

One who has brains enough to tell a man how wonderful he is.

6 Woman's ambition:

To be weighed and found wanting.

7 Worry:

The advance interest you pay on troubles that seldom come.

...Z...

8 Zebra:

A striped horse.

'

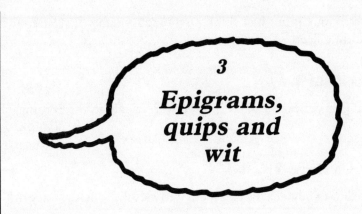

3

Epigrams, quips and wit

1 Everybody Knows This

If nobody knows the trouble you've seen, you don't live in a small town.

2 One Benefit

If you keep your mouth shut, you'll get credit for knowing what you aren't talking about.

3 But You Never Do

Wouldn't it be nice if you could go to the movies and see a picture as good as the one that's coming next week?

4 But It's More Fun

Just about the time a woman thinks her work is all done, she becomes a grandmother.

5 Expensive

Education will never become as expensive as ignorance.

❛ 1 It Could Be Tougher

Life is pretty tough, but just think how much tougher it would be if you couldn't sleep a third of it away.

2 It Seems That Way

The world gets better every day – then worse again in the evening.
Kin Hubbard

3 Most of Us Have Tried

What you don't know makes you look pretty stupid when you try to tell it.

4 In the Minority

The minority is always wrong – at the beginning.

5 How to Lose Friends

The sharp tongue severs many a friendship.

6 Watch It!

If you have a good temper, keep it. If you have a bad temper, don't lose it.

7 Besides, It Helps the Companies

Faith will never die as long as colour seed catalogues are printed.

8 No Trouble

The nice thing about a gift of money is that it's so easy to exchange.

9 Work – a Necessity

Work is a necessity for a man. Man invented the alarm clock.
Pablo Picasso ❜

‘ **1 How You Know**

The man who gives in when he is wrong is wise. The man who gives in when he is right is married.

2 Pretty Expensive

When the philosopher said, 'Hitch your wagon to a star', he had no idea what the space programme would cost.

3 The View Changes

Somehow or other, as we get older, work seems a lot less fun and fun seems a lot more work.

4 Seems Fair

Despite inflation, a penny for some people's thoughts is still a fair price.

5 Exhausted

The average taxpayer is the first of Britain's natural resources to be exhausted.

6 They Soon Learn

Many new fathers soon learn what it means to live in a changing world.

7 Generally

The only things children wear out faster than shoes are parents and teachers.

8 One Advantage

The world changes so fast that a person can't be wrong all the time. ’

'
1 It Might Be

Wouldn't it be simpler to isolate and label the few things that *aren't* harmful to your health?

2 They Can Prove It

Some people have no talent for counting calories – and they have the figures to prove it.

3 Don't Shout

Shouting at children is not the way to make the home a howling success.

4 It Goes Rapidly

About the time one learns how to make the most of life, the most of it is gone.

5 Not Always

There are always two sides to a question – if we aren't involved.

6 It Helps to Know That

Even perfect people buy pencils with rubbers.

7 One Advantage

Keeping your chin up also keeps your mouth closed.

8 Not Now

Can you remember when it was cheaper to park the car than to drive it?
'

1 You Are Also Intact

Stop and let the trains go by –
It hardly takes a minute.
Your car starts out again intact,
And, better still, you're in it.

2 Friction?

Politicians spin their yarns
With smooth and flawless diction,
But one must read between the lines
To sort out truth from fiction.

3 All Her Fault

He wrecked his car, he lost his job, and yet throughout his life he took his troubles like a man – he blamed them on his wife.

4 It's Easy

If you are the kind of person who likes a little free newspaper publicity, just do something stupid.

5 Making a Good Husband

It takes two good women to make a good husband, and the first one is his mother.

6 It Would Be Difficult

The only man who can't change his mind is a man who hasn't got one.

7 Making Progress

Sign on a road: 'If you're lost, just keep on going. You're making good time.'

' **1 Every Year**

We have a neighbour who is a regular churchgoer – never misses an Easter.

2 Don't Wait

If you're going to teach your children the value of a pound, you're going to have to do it awfully fast.

3 Sounds Logical

A lot of trouble in this world is caused by combining a narrow mind with a wide mouth.

4 Keep Out

A passerby read this notice on a farm gate: 'KEEP OUT. Guard dog loose. Survivors will be prosecuted.'

5 Financial Success

The secret of financial success is to spend what you have left after saving, instead of saving what you have left after spending.

6 The Hardest Time

Some people find that the hardest time to get any work done is between coffee breaks.

7 Who Writes the Biography?

Every great man nowadays has his disciples and it is always Judas who writes the biography.   *Oscar Wilde*

8 Say That Again

If our boys and girls are not as good as they were when you were a child their age, it may be that they had a better mother and father than your child has.

'

1 Experience

Experience is a great teacher. A man never wakes his second baby to see it smile.

2 Both Important

Wisdom is divided into two parts: (1) having a great deal to say; (2) not saying it.

3 Especially the Four-wheel Drive

To live in the country one must have the soul of a poet, the mind of a philosopher, the simple tastes of a hermit – and a good four-wheel drive vehicle.

4 New Philosophy

I have a new philosophy. I'm only going to dread one day at a time.
Charles Schulz

5 How Some Drive

Some people drive as if they were anxious to have their accident quickly and get it over with.

' ## 1 It May

Reading made Don Quixote a gentleman, but believing what he read made him mad.   *George Bernard Shaw*

2 How Anger Works

It wouldn't hurt so much to become angry except that, for some reason, anger makes your mouth work faster than your mind.
                                                    Construction Digest

3 Unless

The business of government is to keep the government out of business – that is, unless business needs government aid.

4 Lucky

It's a good thing that beauty is only skin deep, or I'd be rotten to the core.

5 It Sounds That Way

Modern music covers á multitude of dins.

6 Obviously

The man who invented the alarm clock apparently didn't have children.

7 Difficult

It is difficult to believe that someone can differ from us and be right.

8 Some Advice

Don't punch a fellow in the nose when he calls you a fool, unless you think he needs that additional evidence to prove he's right.

9 What People Prefer

People would rather be shown how valuable you are, not told.   '

‘

1 Who Rules the Roost?

When it comes to home rule, Dad may be the chief executive, but Mother is usually the speaker of the house.

2 Seems Doubtful

If your parents didn't have any children, the chances are you won't either.

3 Money

Americans used to shout, 'Give me liberty!' Now they just leave off the last word.

4 It Annoys Us

Have you noticed how close some motorists drive ahead of you?

5 It Could Be

I have always thought of a dog lover as a dog that was in love with another dog.   *James Thurber*

6 Total Stranger

He won't listen to his conscience. He doesn't want advice from a total stranger.

7 Well-to-Do

He looks like a million – after tax.

8 Seventy Years Young

To be seventy years young is sometimes far more cheerful and hopeful than to be forty years old.   *Oliver Wendell Holmes*

9 No Better

Modern art is now being faked, but there is no proof yet that the fake is any better than the original.

’

1 The Land of Opportunity

America is still the land of opportunity where a man can start out digging ditches and wind up behind a desk – if he doesn't mind the financial sacrifice.

2 Not a Little

You can't explode an A-bomb a little.

3 New Books

The worst thing about new books is that they keep us from reading the old ones.

4 What We Believe

Generally the theories we believe we call facts, and the facts we disbelieve we call theories.

5 Correct

Seeing is deceiving. It's eating that's believing.   *James Thurber*

6 Doubt

Even 'yes' men aren't really sure these days.

7 Willing People

The world is full of willing people: some willing to work, the rest willing to let them.

8 Difficult to See

Few people have good enough sight to see their own faults.

9 And to Make a Living

Man invented work as an easy way to escape boredom.

1 Generally

Money isn't everything – sometimes it isn't even enough.

2 Men

I like men to behave like men – strong and childish.

Françoise Sagan

3 No Real Loss

The guy who talks his head off isn't losing much.

4 What the Years Do

Years make all persons old – a few wise.

5 How It Helps

The marvellous thing about a holiday is that it makes you feel good enough to go back to work and poor enough to make you have to.

6 Frankness

Frankness is a virtue, but too much frankness is rudeness.

Gotschal

7 Long Conversations

The longest conversations are usually held by persons with little or nothing to say.

8 Two Views

There are two sides to every story: the book and the movie.

9 He Worked at It

An admirer once asked James Barrie, creator of Peter Pan, how he managed to grow old so gracefully. He answered, 'My dear lady, I give all my time to it.'

1 You Don't Need Manners

Too much of the world is run on the theory that you don't need road manners if you're a five-ton truck.

2 The Worst Moment

The worst moment for the atheist is when he is really thankful and has nobody to thank.　*Dante Gabriel Rossetti*

3 Modern Artists

It is said that some artists paint with one eye shut. Many modern artists shut both eyes.

1 Hiking and Shopping

Men consider a twenty-mile hike exercise. Women call it shopping.

2 Worst Thing About Age

The worst thing about growing old is having to listen to a lot of advice from one's children.

3 What It Reveals

An autobiography usually reveals nothing bad about its writer except his memory.   *Franklin P. Jones*

4 The Voice of Conscience

Those who rarely hear the shrill voice of conscience seem never to miss the faint whisper of temptation.

5 The View Later

Enjoy yourself now. These are the good old days you are going to miss later.

6 Assurance

The wise husband is the one who knows he is right but always asks his wife what she thinks about it.

7 An Advantage

No matter how bad a kid is, he's still good for child benefit.

8 Useful Advice

Cooking hint: The best way to serve spinach is to someone else.

1 Getting Older

A man is getting older when he is going to feel just as well as he ever did in a day or two.

2 When He Doesn't Argue

I never make the mistake of arguing with people for whose opinions I have no respect.   *Edward Gibbon*

3 How People Drive

A great many people drive like tomorrow isn't worth waiting for.

4 It Does Happen

The best blood will sometimes get into a fool or a mosquito.

5 Appreciation

No one is more appreciated that the person who leaves time on the parking meter.

6 It Always Happens

The first one to see a traffic light turn green is the second car back.

7 If

Most people can accept good advice gracefully − if it doesn't interfere with their plans.

8 Don't Hesitate

Don't hesitate to give advice. It passes the time and nobody will follow it anyway.

9 A Good Definition

What is an epigram? a dwarfish whole,
Its body brevity, and wit its soul.

Samuel Taylor Coleridge

'

1 Overheard

I'm going to get out of debt this year if I have to mortgage my house to do it!

2 He Misses the Idea

He misses what is meant by epigram
Who thinks it only frivolous flim-flam.   *Martial*

3 Sound Mind

Being of sound mind, I spent all my money before I died.

4 What They Don't Like

Most people are in favour of progress; it's just the changes that they don't like.

5 Never Welcome, May Be Correct

Advice is seldom welcome; and those who want it the most always like it the least.   *Lord Chesterfield*

6 How to Be Equal

Women will never be men's equals until they can sport a bald spot on top of their heads and still think they're handsome.

7 Seldom Think

The world seems to be full of people who speak twice before they think once.

8 Based on Experience

If someone offers you the world on a platter, take the platter instead.

9 Stubborn

Some minds are like concrete – all mixed up and permanently set.   '

❛ 1 Give Them Time

Nothing's wrong with the younger generation that the older generation didn't outgrow.

2 Even Less Popular

The only person less popular than a wise guy is a wise guy who happens to be right.

3 Even Greater

A learned blockhead is a greater blockhead than an ignorant one.
Benjamin Franklin

4 Listen Carefully

Woman chatting: 'I never repeat gossip, so listen closely now.'

5 But We Don't

It wouldn't be so bad to let one's mind go blank if one always remembered to turn off the sound.

6 It Takes Hard Work

A person has to work himself to death to buy all those labour-saving devices these days.

7 A Hope

The beauty of rearing a large family is that at least one of them may not turn out like the others.

8 Companions

He that lieth down with dogs, shall rise up with fleas.
Benjamin Franklin ❜

‘ 1 More Fun

Living in the past is lots of fun. Besides, it's cheaper.

2 Tact and Truth

Some people have tact; others tell the truth.

3 Two Worries

Two things worry me these days, (1), that things may never get back to normal, and (2), that they already have.

4 Minority Rule

A perfect example of minority rule is a baby in the house.

5 The Truth

I don't care what is written about me so long as it isn't true.
Katharine Hepburn

6 We Need the Diets

Americans have more food to eat than any other people and more diets to keep them from eating it.

7 Exposure

A stitch in time saves embarrassing exposure.

8 The Real Problem

The trouble with being a parent is that by the time you're experienced, you're usually unemployed.

9 The Cost

The best things in life are free. It's the worst things that are so expensive. ’

1 Not Easy

A successful man is one who can earn more than his family can spend.

2 Seems Logical

You ain't learnin' when you're talkin'.   *Lyndon Baines Johnson*

3 One Reason

Figures don't lie – which is one reason why tailoring is so difficult.

4 Almost There Now

Cars are being made that will withstand harder and harder bumps. Pretty soon one will be made that will knock down a pedestrian without jarring the driver.

5 Good Reason

There must have been some reason nature made man's ears to stay open and his mouth to shut.

6 What Man's Inhumanity Does

Man's inhumanity to man makes prizefights, wars and buffet suppers.

7 Optimist

We understand there are some horses that are trained to know that a green light means go and a red light means stop. There may still be hope for some motorists.

8 Never Good

It may be bad to talk when your mouth is full, but it isn't too good either when your head is empty.

1 The Ten Commandments

There are no commandments harder to live by than the first ten.

2 A Good Idea May Run Wild

Even a good idea may run wild in an open and empty mind.

3 The First Rule

The first rule of public speaking is to keep one's mouth shut when one has nothing to say.

4 That's Free

Money will buy a pretty good dog but it won't buy the wag of his tail.   *Josh Billings (Henry Wheeler Shaw)*

5 How Erasmus Spent

When I get a little money, I buy books; and if any is left, I buy food and clothes.   *Erasmus*

6 Or Helsinki

With modern jets, you can experience the thrill of having breakfast in Los Angeles, lunch in New York, dinner in London and baggage in Rome.

7 Wanting Things

I do not read advertisements – I would spend all my time wanting things.   *An Archbishop of Canterbury*

8 Hard to Explain

No one has been able to explain why a child can't walk around a puddle.

1 How to Get Attention

Talk to anyone about himself and he will listen without interrupting.

2 It Doesn't Take Presence

Our experience is that presents make the heart grow fonder.

3 Supply or Demand Side Economics

In a recession, prices are determined by the economic law of over-supply and under-demand.

4 What's Wrong

The only thing wrong with the world is people.

5 They All Have Budget Deficits

Every nation finds it difficult to balance a budget at the end of the sword.

6 Interest on a Loan

Interest on a loan may be so high that if you can afford to pay it, you don't need the loan.

7 Fooling Himself

The person who thinks he is fooling everyone but himself is nearsighted.

8 It Pays to Remember

A short speech may not be the best speech, but the best speech is a short one.

9 It Works

There is no cure for insomnia like listening to yourself talk.

1 The Stork's Bill

No bird has a bill as long as the stork's.

2 It Helps

Poor memory has its benefits. Otherwise a person would remember the times he has been a fool.

3 The Difference

The American public spends more money on chewing gum than on books. But after all, you can borrow a book.

4 Social Insects

An author recently wrote a book called *Social Insects*. All of us know some he never met.

5 The Pedestrian

Every year is leap year for the pedestrian.

❮ 1 It Is Sometimes Discouraging

The thing that is discouraging about spring is that everything seems to come back but us.

2 Is This Clear?

When you hear one person talk about what he does not understand to another person who doesn't understand him, that is economics.

3 What Bothers You

It may be your winter underwear and not your conscience that bothers you.

4 How Could They?

Husbands don't tell their wives everything. After all, there are only twenty-four hours in a day.

5 The Religion Some People Want

Some people want a religion that will make them feel respectable but not require them to be.

6 He Has to Be Careful

A man never knows how careful he can be until he puts on a white summer outfit.

7 You Can't Win

When you go back to your old home town, you will find half the people don't remember you and the other half don't know you've been away.

8 Liars Also Figure

Figures don't lie, but a lot of lying can be done with them. ❯

1 Each One Writes a Book

We admire the courage of the retired generals and politicians who decide that now it can be told – at £5 a word.

2 Our Deficits

A balance of payments deficit is bad, but it's comforting to have at least one thing that's permanent and unchanging.

3 Related

The USSR and China may be brothers, but so were the James boys.

4 Unfortunate

Pity the person who has insomnia so badly he can't even sleep in the office.

5 It's Also an Asset

Every now and then you find a woman who can dish it out better than she can cook.

6 Little Conviction

It isn't how much thought went into developing television that determines how much thought now comes out of it.

7 The Designs Are Permanent

Women's styles change far more frequently than their designs.

8 Fortunate

No two persons are alike, and most of them are glad of it.

9 It Depends

Whether a pedestrian gets an even break depends on just how he was hit.

‘ 1 Great Achievement

It is no great thing to be humble when you are brought low; but to be humble when you are praised is a great and rare attainment.

2 Not New

If at first you don't succeed, you're like everyone else.

3 Very Tiresome

Doing nothing is the most tiresome job in the world because you can't stop and rest.

4 A Real Friend

He is the kind of a friend you can depend on – always around when he needs you.

5 Advice

Former New York Mayor LaGuardia to reporters: 'Be sure you have your facts straight before you distort them.'

6 Act Now

You cannot do a kindness too soon, because you never know how soon it will be too late.

7 Be Very Careful

Children should be very careful what they say. Parents are always repeating what they hear.

8 Similar

Young people are alike these days in many disrespects.

9 Right

Most people can keep a secret; it's the people they tell it to who can't. ’

1 We're All There Now

An Englishman can consider himself a success when it costs him more to support his government than his family.

2 They're Probably Happier

The reason most people know little about what's going on in the world is that this information isn't found in the comic strips.

3 Worth It

Much advice may be had for nothing – and usually it's worth it.

4 Don't Look

Where did you get the idea that swimming is good for the figure? Did you ever take a good look at a whale?

5 That Helps

Listening to advice may get you into trouble, but it makes the other person feel better.

6 Intuition

Intuition is what enables a woman to contradict her husband before he says anything.

7 We All Are

The easiest thing in the world is to convince a person that he is overworked.

8 He Has It

A tax collector has what it takes to take what you've got.

9 It Doesn't Take Long

A fool and his money are soon invited places.

1 Happens to Everyone

It used to be that a fool and his money were soon parted, but now it happens to everybody.

2 Great Puzzle

One of the greatest puzzles is how the fool and his money got together in the first place.

3 Badly Needed

What we need is a car you can drive to the office or shops and then fold up and carry with you.

1 It's Different Now

In the modern family, the daughters don't live at home until after they're married.

2 They Tell Your Fortune

There's no fortune teller like Dun & Bradstreet.

3 The Reason

The reason history has to repeat itself is that no one heard it the first time.

4 Worth It

If you lend someone £10 and don't see him again, it may be worth it.

5 Tax Increases and Tax Cuts

Any government avoids a tax increase just before an election or a tax cut just after an election.

6 Not Confused

A man never gets so confused in his thinking that he can't see the other fellow's duty.

7 Good Suggestion

Sometimes it is better to put off until tomorrow what you are likely to botch today.

8 Surprised

Behind every successful man stands a surprised mother-in-law.

9 Efficient

The only person ever to get his work done by Friday was Robinson Crusoe.

1 Only One Thing Left

After paying for the wedding, about the only thing a father has left to give away is the bride.

2 Punctuality

Punctuality is the art of guessing how late the other guy will be.

3 It Can't Be Done

He travels faster who has the ability to fold road maps.

4 Only One Worry

Historians tell us about the past and economists about the future. Only the present is confusing.

5 Lost in Thought

Too often the person who gets lost in thought does so because it's unfamiliar territory.

6 Following Our Example

Children are creatures who disgrace you by exhibiting in public the example you set for them at home.

7 They Learn the Tricks

Some persons are so busy learning the tricks of the trade that they never learn the trade.

8 It Isn't Easy Here Either

Some think that the moon won't be able to support life. Well, it's not such an easy thing on this old planet either.

9 One Advantage

Slang has this advantage over pure English: when you use it, most people understand exactly what you mean.

1 The Right Place

Sign in optician's window: 'If you don't see what you want, you've come to the right place.'

2 Can't Keep Quiet

An egotist is usually me-deep in conversation.

3 It Helps

If at first you don't succeed, try looking in the waste paper basket for the directions.

4 Handicap

It's tough on a woman who wants to make a success in business; she doesn't have a wife to advise her.

5 Don't Hesitate

He who hesitates misses the green light, gets bumped in the rear, and loses his parking place.

6 Hard to Realize

It's a terrible shock for most of us to find out that you can't economize without spending less money.

7 Don't Worry

If you fool some of the people all of the time, and all of the people some of the time, you need not worry; someone else will fool them the rest of the time.

8 Distributing Wealth

Nothing redistributes wealth like taxation and a big family.

' 1 Why Governments Change

No leftist party stays in power long in any country because it must get out occasionally to let the conservatives pay the debts.

2 Wisdom

No one becomes wise who is sure he already is.

3 Can't Recall

Have you ever seen a jogger smile?

4 Changing Times

Old man: One who remembers when the moon inspired only romance instead of space travel.

5 At the Fountain of Knowledge

Some students drink deeply at the fountain of knowledge – others only gargle.

6 Listen

There is only one rule for being a good talker: learn to listen.

7 What It Shows

Early to bed and early to rise is a sure sign that you don't care for television.

8 Forget It

Don't worry if you start losing your memory. Just forget about it.

9 Willing

Everybody is willing to forget the past if it catches up with them. **'**

1 It Isn't Easy

The goal of some ambitious people is not to be somebody, but to do somebody.

2 Naturally

Sign in a shop window: 'We buy old furniture. We sell antiques.'

3 Pride

The less a person has – even brains – the prouder he is of it.

4 Labour-saving

One of the greatest labour-saving devices of today is called tomorrow.

5 Inside Information

Never argue with your doctor; he has inside information.

6 Don't Go Too Far

It's smart to pick your friends, but not to pieces.

7 Elections

Some elections don't prove the people aren't conservative. They only prove that they don't get mad when they're prosperous.

8 Hard Lesson

The greatest boon to this generation financially was learning to spend the income of the next generation.

9 Gossip

For gossip to succeed, it has to be unreasonable enough to shock everyone and reasonable enough that a few will believe it.

'

1 One Advantage

One of the nicest features about old age is that you can whistle while you brush your teeth.

2 Simple

This fishing business is simple – all you have to do is get there yesterday when the fish were biting.

3 Our Worry

What's worrying us is that the government is living not only beyond its own income but also beyond ours.

4 That's Different

When you have to swallow your own medicine, the spoon seems very large.

5 Exercise

The only exercise some people get is jumping to conclusions, running down friends, sidestepping responsibility, and pushing their luck.

6 Changes Your View

Nothing makes you more tolerant of a neighbour's noisy party than being there.

7 Service

Sign in a pawnshop window: 'See us at your earliest inconvenience.'

8 Correct

Freudian news misprint: 'The motorist approached the coroner at ninety miles per hour.'

'

1 Comfortably Unhappy

Money may not buy happiness, but with it you can be unhappy in perfect comfort.

2 Easier

It is much easier to be critical than correct.

3 The Computer

The computer is a moron.   *Peter Drucker*

4 It Took Practice

A person who is a good liar got that way by long practice.

5 It's Wise to Jump

He is the kind of person who makes others jump – a reckless driver.

6 They Don't Need To

Money talks, but the folks who know how to save it don't.

7 Or Get a Different House

People who live in glass houses might as well answer the doorbell.

8 Might Help

All the world needs is an agreement not to have any more wars until the old ones are paid for.

9 Lazy Not Wise

Early to bed and late to rise.
Makes one lazy rather than wise.

' **1 Not Exciting**

One way to avoid excitement is to live within your income.

2 Too Fidgety

Many a fellow gets a reputation for being energetic when in truth he is merely fidgety.

3 Getting Attention

The quickest way to get someone's undivided attention is to make a mistake.

4 Helping Fix Things

For fixing things around the house, nothing beats a chequebook.

5 A Real Executive

A real executive is one who trains others to handle his responsibilities.

6 Be Thrifty Anyway

Be thrifty when you're young, and when you're old you'll be able to afford the things that only the young can enjoy.

7 Make Others Happy

Never miss an opportunity to make others happy, even if you have to leave them alone to do it.

8 One Advantage

There is one thing that can be said about ignorance: it causes a lot of interesting arguments.

9 One Test

You are getting old if it takes you longer to rest than it did to get tired. **'**

1 High Face Value

A smile can add a great deal to one's face value.

2 You Have to Hurry

If you think twice before you speak, you'll never get into the conversation.

3 A Prescription

'What this country needs,' said a prominent medical man, 'is tranquillity without tranquillizers.'

4 Could Talk Forever

Though I'm anything but clever,
I could talk like that forever.   *W. S. Gilbert*

5 Can't Understand

I have never been able to understand why it is that just because I am unintelligible nobody understands me.

6 Is That Clear?

Be obscure clearly.

7 Not Strange

The average man seems able to detect a rattle in his car more quickly than one in his head.

8 One Good Point

A conceited person has at least one good point: he doesn't talk about other people.

9 Even a Small One

Most arguments about new cars start from scratch.

' **1 Increasing Enthusiasm**

Nothing increases your enthusiasm like having your own way.

2 Too True

A man begins cutting his wisdom teeth the first time he bites off more than he can chew.

3 Three Kinds of People

There are three kinds of people: the few who make things happen, the many who watch things happen, and those who have no idea what has happened.

4 A Right to His Opinion

Always be tolerant of a person who disagrees with you. After all, he has a right to his ridiculous opinion.

5 Keep Smiling

Keep smiling. It makes everyone wonder what you've been up to.

6 Playing It Safe

People don't always believe everything they hear, but often they repeat it just to be on the safe side.

7 What It Indicates

A chip on the shoulder indicates that there's wood higher up.

8 One Thing He Needs

For the man who has everything: a calendar to remind him when the payments are due.

9 It Helps

More doors are opened with 'please' than with keys.

1 One Advantage

Laugh at 'puppy love' if you like, but it's the only thing that can reconcile a boy to washing his neck and ears.

2 She Probably Did

The man who boasts he never made a mistake in his life may have a wife who did.

3 Gets Worse

Work may not be as hard as it used to be, but it is certainly more taxing.

4 Works Both Ways

The driver is safer when the roads are dry; the roads are safer when the driver is dry.

5 Helpful

A nice thing about a one-way street is that you can only get bumped in the rear.

'

1 Besides Money

Money isn't everything. After all, there are cheques, charge accounts and credit cards.

2 Unusual Problem

The dear old lady expressed the spirit of the day, whether intentionally or unintentionally, when she said that she could get along very well without the necessities of life, but she just couldn't be reconciled to getting along without the luxuries.

3 Solved Hard Problem

It is reported that a young student recently stayed up all night figuring out what became of the sun when it went down. It finally dawned on him.

4 Lucky

Confucius say: 'Man in barrel is lucky – to still have barrel.'

5 Helpful

The trouble is that one extravagance always suggests another.

6 We Agree

Most people think they would rather be miserably rich than happily poor.

7 Improves with Time

Your temper is one of the few things that improves the longer you keep it.

8 Gratitude

Says the habitual borrower: 'Lend me £10 and I'll be everlastingly in your debt.'

'

1 At Least It's Done

After you decide that nothing can be done, someone comes along and does it.

2 Same Objective

Many of us live expensively to impress our friends who live expensively to impress us.

3 How to Get Ahead

Some people would get along better financially by spending less money than they haven't earned, for things they don't need, to impress people they don't like.

4 Advice to Lawyers

If you have the law on your side, address the court; if you have the facts on your side address the jury; but if you have neither the law nor the facts, abuse the other side.

5 Occasionally

The person who does a lot of talking is bound to be right – some time.

6 Not Easy

Few of us can stand prosperity. Another man's, I mean.

Mark Twain

7 Learning by Doing

If we learn by doing things, a lot of people are going to keep on being ignorant.

8 What They Discover

When a man and woman marry they become one, and then they discover which one.

1 That's Our Experience

Shake and shake the ketchup bottle.
None will come, and then a lot'll.

2 Absent-minded

Did you hear the one about the absent-minded motorist who changed his oil every day and his shirt every 2,000 miles?

3 Thankful

Perhaps we ought to be thankful to the fellow who keeps us so busy listening to his troubles that we haven't time to think of our own.

4 She Ain't Benzine

Mary had a little lamp,
She filled it with benzine;
She went to light her little lamp,
And hasn't since benzine.

5 They Fall in the Fall

The autumn leaves are falling, are falling here and there.
They're falling through the atmosphere, and also through the air.

6 More Expensive Too

We have discovered that family ties are stronger at Christmas-time – and louder, too.

7 Too Bad

The church bell is far more important than the fire bell, but it does not make the people run nearly so fast.

8 Criticism

Criticism is one of the few things people would rather give than take.

1 Usually

Those rainy days for which a man saves usually come during his holiday.

2 No Use Trying

Dignity is a thing that can't be preserved in alcohol.

3 Wise Decision

A teenager always reaches for a chair when she answers the telephone.

4 Leaves No Impression

A shallow thinker seldom makes a deep impression.

5 Laughable Argument

If both sides of an argument make you laugh, you are either broad-minded or stupid.

6 Serving Self Only

Too many of us conduct our lives on the cafeteria plan: self-service only.

7 One Advantage

The wonderful thing about a dull party is that you can get home early.

8 Economics Lesson

The reason talk is cheap is that the supply always exceeds the demand.

9 Helpful

It is always easier to arrive at a firm conviction about a problem after you know what the boss thinks.

' **1 A Jefferson Invention**

Thomas Jefferson invented the swivel chair, which showed how well he knew bureaucrats.

2 Or Vice Versa

Leisure time is when your wife can't find you.

3 Keeping It Working

Even when a marriage is made in heaven, the maintenance work has to be done on earth.

4 An Idea

Someone should invent a car with brakes that will get tight when the driver does!

5 Night Driving

The increase in car accidents late at night is due to a combination of head lights and light heads.

6 An Uplifter

One of the world's greatest uplifters is the alarm clock.

7 Doctor's Instructions

If you're thin, the doctor says, 'Don't eat fast.' If you're fat, he says, 'Don't eat. Fast.'

8 It Doesn't Help

The only people who listen to both sides of an argument are the next-door neighbours.

9 You Said It

There are bigger things in life than money: bills.

'

1 A Struggle

Life is a struggle to keep earning capacity up with yearning capacity.

2 Human Error

To err is only human, but when you wear out the rubber before you've used up the pencil, you're overdoing it.

3 It Helps

Nature couldn't make us perfect, so she did the next best thing – she made us blind to our faults.

4 Hard to Explain

If you don't believe in luck, how else do you explain the success of those you don't like?

5 Think About This

Don't finish anything you aren't able to start.

6 Upsetting

Nothing is so upsetting to a person as to have company drop in to see the house looking like it usually does.

7 Truth in Advertising

A plaque on the wall of a psychiatrist's office: 'No one in his right mind ever comes to see me.'

8 This Is Fame

An architect once designed a building so beautiful that other architects admired it.

9 Line Is Often Busy

The line is too often busy when conscience wishes to speak.

' **1 Gossip**

Gossip goes in both ears and comes out of the mouth greatly enlarged.

2 Plagiarism

A plagiarist is a person who improves on something that was poorly written.

3 Nash Nuances

I would live all my life in nonchalance and insouciance were it not for making a living, which is rather a nouciance.   *Ogden Nash*

4 American Families

The thing that impresses me most about America is the way parents obey their children.   *Edward, Duke of Windsor, 1957*

5 Pedestrians

A zombie has no mind of his own and walks around without knowing where he's going or what he's doing. . . . In Hollywood they call them 'pedestrians'.   *Bob Hope*

6 Education

When a subject becomes totally obsolete we make it a required course.

7 Infancy

Infancy is the period of our lives when, according to Wordsworth, 'Heaven lies about us.' The world begins lying about us pretty soon afterwards.   *Ambrose Bierce*

8 No Influence

If you think you have influence, just try ordering somebody else's dog around.   '

1 Similes Can Be Humorous and Wise

No more social position than an onion.
A night as cold and damp as a dog's nose.
Frivolous as meringue.
Useless as a pulled tooth.
Mysterious as chop suey.
In her single person she managed to produce the effect of a majority.
No more sense of direction than a bunch of firecrackers.

2 Use Metaphors in Speech and Conversation

He nudged me with a wink.
He strains his conversation through a cigar.
She's the plot of his life's story.
She shifted her face into neutral.
The general creased a little in the middle to signify he was bowing.
Streets mushroomed with umbrellas.
I buttoned up the pockets of my sympathy.

3 They Never Die

Old college deans never die – they only lose their faculties.
Old politicians never die – they just run once too often.
Old volcanoes never die – they just blow their tops.
Old cows never die – they just kick the bucket.
Old farmers never die – they just go to seed.
Old silencers never die – they just get exhausted.
Old bankers never die – they just lose interest.

4 Saving Time

Every busy man should have a wife, so he won't need to waste so much time making up his mind about things.

5 Think Twice

Before criticizing your wife's faults, remember that it may have been those very defects that prevented her from catching a better husband.

6 A Wrong Number?

Uneasy lies the head that ignores a telephone call at night.

❛ 1 Easier

It's far easier to forgive an enemy after you've got even with him.

2 It Isn't Enough

A liar needs a good memory.   *Quintilian*

3 Practical Idea

Why doesn't somebody cross electric blankets with toasters so that people could pop out of bed early each morning?

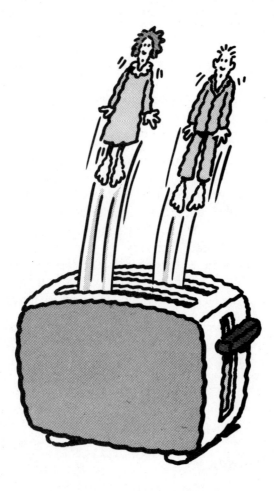

❜

1 Not an Authority

A comedian says people do not appreciate new jokes. How would he know?

2 They Can't Help It

A scientist says a great many animals laugh. How can they help it when they watch what people do?

3 Covering Up

Architects cover their mistakes with ivy. Lawyers visit theirs in jail. Advertising executives put theirs on television. And cooks cover theirs with mayonnaise.

4 Yes!

Are you in favour of progress, just so long as nobody changes anything?

5 Naturally

Why was King Arthur's time called the Dark Ages? Because there were so many knights.

6 Tough Luck

A small boy defined 'mixed emotions' as a morning when the local radio station tells you school is closed because of a power cut – and you're in bed with the flu.

7 Under Her Direction

A woman never really makes a fool of a man – she merely directs the performance.

8 A Dead Cert

To get nothing for something, bet on the horses or on any sure thing.

' 1 What the Schoolboy Thought

Trigonometry is having three wives at one time, according to one twelve-year-old.

2 Inevitable

Many famous persons sooner or later write their alibiography.

3 Hard to Explain

Why is it that the wrong number on a telephone is never busy when you call?

4 Common Experience

Many a wife has helped her husband to the top of the ladder – and left him there while she tried to make up her mind whether the picture would look better there, or somewhere else.

5 Get Your Mouth Round That

Spoonerisms (misplaced letters or syllables in two or more words): 'Half-warmed fish' for 'half-formed wish'.

Reverend William A. Spooner

A drama critic is a man who leaves no turn unstoned.

George Bernard Shaw

6 A Clear Case for a Dictionary

Malapropisms (word misused by someone attempting to appear learned):
He took the alligator to the top of the building.
She has a nice sense of rumour.
It was a case of mistaken nonentity.
She picked a lawyer out of the phone book at ransom.
My husband doesn't munch words! **'**

' **1 Dangerous**

Who ever heard of fat men heading a riot, or herding together in turbulent mobs? No, 'tis your lean, hungry men who are continually worrying society, and setting the whole community by the ears.

Washington Irving

2 Popularized

Some historians say the Egyptians contributed more to civilization than any other people – they invented and popularized soap.

3 Maybe

I always make it a point to speak grammatically. Who knows? It might become popular again.   *Bette Davis*

4 The Way it Starts

How a family starts – it starts with a young man falling in love with a girl. No superior alternative has yet been found.

Winston Churchill

,

' 1 It Evens Out

Things are pretty well evened up in this world. Other people's troubles are not as bad as yours, but their children are a lot worse.

2 One Match

One tree can make a million matches. One match can destroy a million trees.

3 Keep It Quiet

The ancient sage who concocted the maxim 'Know Thyself' might have added, 'Don't Tell Anyone!'

4 Humour

Humour makes the educated mind a safer mind.

5 A Real Problem

A bus driver said he could not stay on schedule if he had to keep on picking up passengers.

6 Confident

What makes an economic forecaster confident? No one else knows anything about the future either.

7 Never Loses

What person never loses an argument? A traffic policeman.

8 Higher Standard

I am different from Washington; I have a higher, grander standard of principle. Washington could not lie. I can lie, but I won't.

Mark Twain '

4 Did you know these facts?

1 Latin America's Growth

By the year 2000, Latin America's teeming millions may be exceeded only by those of Asia. If the present growth trend continues to the end of the century, Latin America will have almost twice as many people as the United States and Canada.

2 Alphabets of Various Nations

The alphabets of different languages contain the following number of letters: English, 26; French, 23; Italian, 20; Spanish, 27; German, 26; Slavonic, 27; Russian, 41; Latin, 22; Greek, 24; Hebrew, 22; Arabic, 28; Persian, 32; Turkish, 33; Sanskrit, 50.
Pity the poor Chinese! To read intelligently, they must learn at least 3,000 characters. And that isn't all! Wise Chinese must know at least 40,000 characters.

3 Sold for Just $400!

The name of Walter Hunt, inventor of the safety pin, is little known. In 1849, ten years before he died, Hunt began fiddling with a little piece of wire, developed a safety pin and finally sold the idea for just $400, which is all he ever made from the invention.

163

6 **1 How Long Animals Live**

How would birds and animals look on birthdays if they knew when theirs came around? Of all the birds, swans have the most birthdays; they have been known to live 300 years.

Among animals, whales are entitled to the most birthday cake candles. Their average lifespan is about 1,000 years. The whales that follow ships in the Atlantic today also followed the little ships in Columbus's small fleet back in 1492.

Elephants, under good conditions, will live 400 years.
Tortoises have many birthdays too. They live considerably past 100 years.

The average number of birthdays of horses is 25 to 30; and of pigs, 20. Of the smaller animals, dogs and cats usually have 10 to 15 birthdays, and squirrels and rabbits 7 or 8.

2 How It Started

James Watt, the Scottish inventor who built the first steam engine, also named its energy – horsepower. This term was necessary, for there was no other way for people to understand or measure the power of the steam engine. So, Watt, with a mature horse, rope and pulleys, determined how much weight the horse could lift in a minute – a 3,300-pound weight to a height of 10 feet in one minute.

Then Watt discovered that his steam engine could lift a 3,300-pound weight to a height of 100 feet. Thus, the steam engine provided ten times as much power as one mature horse. Watt termed his machine a 10-horsepower engine. And horsepower is still the measurement for petrol engines, diesel engines, electric motors and even atomic reactors.   *Good Reading*

3 A Major Decision

It was in 1867 that William Seward, then US Secretary of State, persuaded an reluctant Congress to ratify the treaty with Russia that made Alaska a possession of the United States. The purchase price of $7,200,000 was considered exorbitant, even though it worked out to about $12 per square mile or less than 2 cents an acre. On discovery of the gold fields in the 1880s, Seward's Folly was acknowledged as a masterpiece of foresightedness.   **9**

' **1 There Is Hope for Everyone**

The garlic plant belongs to the lily family.

2 Is That Clear?

A Louisiana lawyer, hired by a New York firm to trace the abstract of a deed, went back to 1803, the year Louisiana was purchased from France. Then the firm wrote to the lawyer saying that he would have to trace the ownership of the land further back than that. In due time he did so, reporting by letter as follows:

'Dear Sirs: I traced your deed back to 1803. Here it is complete. As you probably know, Louisiana was purchased from France in 1803; France had acquired Louisiana from the Spanish as the result of a successful war against the Spaniards. The Spaniards acquired Louisiana as the result of the explorations of an Italian named Columbus. Columbus was financially backed by Isabella and Ferdinand of Spain. They were given permission for Columbus's expedition by the Pope. The Pope is the vicar of Christ. Christ is the Son of God. God made Louisiana!'

3 How Prophetic!

In 1894, when there were only four cars in the United Staes, a New York publisher brought out the first issue of the *Horseless Age*, a trade magazine, which contained this prophetic statement: 'Those who have taken the pains to search beneath the surface for the great tendencies of the age see what a giant industry is struggling into being.

'

‘ 1 It Wasn't Easy Either

Tennis was originally played without racquets. Players hit the ball over the net with the palms of their hands.

2 If Any Creatures Are Looking

If there were creatures on Mars using telescopes to study the earth, the first evidence of life they would see is the Great Wall of China because it is the largest structure ever built on our globe. Made of bricks nearly 2,200 years ago, it is 1,500 miles long from Kiangsu to the sea, varies from 18 to 35 feet high, and is thick enough for a road on top. It cost the lives of an estimated 400,000 workers, many of whom were buried inside the wall, which has been called 'the longest cemetery in the world'.

3 Some Do Even More

According to one statistician, the average person spends at least thirteen years of his or her life talking. On a normal day, about 18,000 words are likely to be used − roughly the equivalent of a book of 54 pages. In the course of a single year, your words would fill 66 books, each book containing 800 pages.

4 It Was No Joke to Him

It was a joke that had been tried on every embryonic engineer since the electric light was hardly a gleam in Edison's brain. The novice engineer would be assigned the 'impossible' task of frosting electric light bulbs on the inside.

A new engineer at General Electric, Marvin Pipkin, was put through the usual routine. In all innocence Pipkin discovered a way not only to frost bulbs on the inside but also to etch the glass with soft, rounded pits which gave the bulbs added strength and effected maximum diffusion of the light.

Fortunately no one told him that he had been assigned the impossible, so he went ahead and accomplished it!

Executives' Digest **’**

1 It Looked Large Then

Edgar Allan Poe was not a successful author in his lifetime. When he finally sold his now famous poem 'The Raven', he was paid $10 for it. Now the original manuscript is valued at $250,000.

2 Who Said It?

Here are some common phrases used every day. See if you have any idea where they came from:
'Thanks for nothing.'
'No limits but the sky.'
'To give the devil his due.'
'A peck of troubles.'
'Let the worst come to the worst.'
'A finger in every pie.'
'Every dog has his day.'
'A wild goose chase.'
Give up? Every one of these phrases appeared in one book, *Don Quixote,* written more than 350 years ago by Miguel de Cervantes.

3 They Make All the Picnics

In proportion to its size, the ant has the largest brain in the animal kingdom.

4 Young Geniuses

Thomas Jefferson wrote the Declaration of Independence when he was thirty-three.

Chaucer was well known at court as a poet when he was but twenty-five.

Livy began his *History of Rome* at the age of twenty-four.

Molière finished a comedy, his best, at seventeen.

Milton wrote 'Comus', esteemed by some as one of his most charming poems, at twenty-six.

Keats made himself immortal in English literature before his death at twenty-four.

Beethoven was a skilled composer at nineteen.

Henry Ford started developing his first car while in his thirties.

Edison invented the incandescent electric light when he was only thirty-two.

' 1 Exodus of 2 Million

Historians claim that Moses led more than 2 million people out of Egypt in that historic exodus.

2 Accidental

Alexander Graham Bell was trying to devise a hearing aid for his wife when he accidentally invented the telephone.

3 Almost Speechless

There are more than 400,000 words in the English language; the average person knows or can use less than 3 per cent of them. Even journalists are able to use only about 20,000 words, only 5 per cent of the total number.

1 A 'Vertical' River

The most vertical river in the world is the Jordan. In a little more than one hundred miles, it drops from 1,700 feet above sea level to 1,300 feet below. Nothing on this planet compares with the River Jordan.

From its source in the springs of Mount Hermon, it winds so much that its flowing distance is over 200 miles – more than twice the distance as the crow flies. After about 35 miles, it has dropped from a height of 1,700 feet to sea level. Then for 10 miles it plunges through cataracts and whirlpools, and pours into the Sea of Galilee nearly 700 feet below the level of the sea.

It rushes through the Sea of Galilee so rapidly that its waters do not mingle with it, even though that lake is 14 miles long. Then it keeps tumbling and rushing through huge gorges for over 100 miles towards the Dead Sea. There it reaches its lowest point, 1,300 feet below sea level.

The land adjoining is the lowest land area in the world. Death Valley in California – the deepest in America – only reaches a level of 276 feet below the sea.

The salty Dead Sea into which the Jordan empties is in some places 1,300 feet deep. The bottom of the Dead Sea is the deepest natural hole in this earth, measuring about half a mile below the level of the sea.   *Sunshine Magazine*

2 In Old School Days

Times have changed. If you don't believe it, read the following rules that were in force at a well-known seat of higher learning for young American women, Mount Holyoke College, in 1837:

'No young lady shall become a member of Mt Holyoke Seminary who cannot kindle a fire, mash potatoes, and repeat the multiplication table and at least two-thirds of the shorter catechism.

'Every member of the school shall walk a mile a day unless . . . earthquake, or some other calamity prevent.

'No young lady shall devote more than an hour a day to miscellaneous reading.

'No young lady is expected to have gentlemen acquaintances unless they are returned missionaries or agents of benevolent societies.'

‘ ## 1 The Mysteries of Nature

The speed of American monarch butterflies has been recorded at about 10 miles per hour when they are cruising, but they can sprint as fast as 30 miles per hour. One tagged butterfly was captured, released and captured again, recording a flight of 80 miles in one day. The longest recorded flight of a monarch was 1,870 miles from Toronto in Canada, to San Luis Potosi in Mexico.

2 Valuable Information

While eating a typical dinner, the average person swallows 295 times.

3 It Ain't Necessarily So

Sometimes what most people think is the truth 'ain't necessarily so'. For example, most Americans probably think Portland Cement comes from Portland, Oregon, or perhaps from Portland, Maine. But it doesn't come from Portland anywhere. It merely looks like Portland stone, which comes from England.

Most people know that chop suey is a Chinese dish and logically should come from China, but it doesn't. It was invented in Brooklyn, New York, and even then not by a Chinese cook but by an Italian. And the world-famous Italian dish spaghetti isn't really Italian in origin. It was brought from China to Italy by the explorer Marco Polo.

Additionally, many people would seriously question your intelligence if you said that tomatoes, bananas and pineapples are berries – but berries they are.

4 He Liked Himself?

The Dutch artist Rembrandt painted sixty-two self-portraits.

’

‘

5
Stories and comments from famous and unusual lives

1 Hardship

Alexander Pope, the famous poet (1688–1744), who was the first English writer to make money from his work, was only 4 feet 6 inches tall, suffered from poor health most of his life, and was so frail that he had to wear a corset in order to stand upright.

2 Stay in College

World-famous boxer Muhammad Ali was once asked by a young man what he should do with his life. The heavyweight's reply was, 'Stay in college, get the knowledge. And stay there until you're through. If they can make penicillin out of mouldy bread, they can sure make something out of you!'

3 Being Wholly Alive

I wouldn't swap one wrinkle of my face for all the elixirs of youth. all of these wrinkles represent a smile, a grimace of pain and disappointment...some part of being fully alive.

Helen Hayes ’

(**1 Not Too Bad**

Many years ago an Englishwoman, perhaps a little envious, told James McNeill Whistler that she thought the politeness of the French was all on the surface. The artist replied: 'That is a very good place for it to be.'

2 Sad If True

The historian Arnold Toynbee said: 'Of the twenty-two civilizations that appear in history, nineteen of them collapsed when they reached the moral state the United States is in now.'

3 The Time Will Come

Once the great Lord Melbourne, then Prime Minister, asked a young man named Disraeli what he would like to be. Disraeli boldly replied, 'Prime Minister of England'. Few men in world history present a more remarkable illustration of the ability to overcome hardship than Disraeli. His Jewish background at first made him unacceptable to the higher echelons of society at that time. Three times he was defeated in parliamentary elections. When he made his first speech in the House of Commons he was ridiculed, hissed and jeered. He cried out, 'The time will come when you will hear me.' And the time did come. He was determined. With courage and confidence he fought his way from the back benches of the House of Commons to become Prime Minister of the British Empire.

4 A Businessman's Philosophy

The well-known American store owner and entrepreneur Marshall Field once said, 'Each and every man ought to interest himself in public affairs. There's no happiness in mere dollars. After they are acquired, one can use but a very moderate amount. It is given a man to eat so much, to wear so much, and to have so much shelter, and more he cannot use. When money has supplied these, its mission, so far as the individual is concerned, is fulfilled, and a man must look still further and higher. It is only in wide public affairs, where money is a moving force toward the general welfare, that the possessor of it can possibly find pleasure and that only in constantly doing more. The greatest good a man can do is to cultivate himself, develop his) 'talents and powers in order that he may be of greater service to humanity.'

1 Sound Values

Marshall Field once set out the following 12 reminders that can be helpful in obtaining a sound sense of values:

The value of time.
The success of perseverance.
The pleasure of working.
The dignity of simplicity.
The worth of character.
The power of kindness.
The influence of example.
The obligation of duty.
The wisdom of economy.
The virtue of patience.
The improvement of talent.
The joy of originating.

2 Something for Everybody

Like other US Presidents and Statesmen everywhere, Abraham Lincoln suffered from the importunities of job seekers and persons looking for special favours, which once drove him to ask his doctor where he could get smallpox. 'Then,' he said, 'I shall have something I can give to everybody.'

3 When We Pray

It is for us to pray not for tasks equal to our powers, but for powers equal to our tasks; to go forward with a great desire forever beating at the door of our hearts as we travel toward our distant goal.

Helen Keller

4 History

The brilliant leader and military strategist Napoleon was 'Waterlooed' by the middle-aged son of an English musician, voted by his classmates at Eton as the 'boy least likely to do anything'.'

' **1 Efficiency**

Napoleon is reported to have had a rule that none of his incoming mail was to be opened for a period of three weeks, on the theory that most of the problems they raised would have solved themselves in that time.

2 How to Give Advice

I have found the best way to give advice to your children is to find out what they want and then advise them to do it.

Harry S Truman

3 Your Obligation

People owe this marvellous world whatever talents they can give it. They owe enough to the world to be a part of it, to use their talents to make others happy.   *Mary Martin*

4 It Never Happened

When I look back on all these worries, I remember the story of the old man who said, on his deathbed, that he had a lot of trouble in his life, most of which never happened.   *Winston Churchill*

5 God in Every Person

I believe that God is in every person, and therefore, I don't get angry with people and I don't hate people. If something bad happens – I forget it right away, or at least ten minutes later.   *George Burns*

6 Could This Happen?

I believe that the heaviest blow ever dealt at liberty's head will be dealt by this nation [the United States] in the ultimate failure of its example to the earth.   *Charles Dickens*

7 How to Honour Christmas

I will honour Christmas in my heart, and try to keep it all the year.

Charles Dickens **'**

1 Real Fiction

Income tax returns are the most imaginative fiction being written today.   *Herman Wouk*

2 They Came Earlier

My folks didn't come over on the *Mayflower,* but they were here to meet the boat.   *Will Rogers*

3 What Turns Up

When you're down and out, something always turns up – and it's usually the noses of your friends.   *Orson Welles*

4 Those Who Dream

It may be those who do most, dream most.   *Stephen Leacock*

5 Disappointment

Anyone who expects something for nothing is all the better for being disappointed, because he learns something.   *Henry Ford*

6 An Architect's Mistakes

A doctor can bury his mistakes but an architect can only advise his client to plant vines.   *Frank Lloyd Wright*

7 Humility

Don't be humble. You're not that great.   *Golda Meir*

8 Learning about Yourself

You learn more about yourself campaigning for just one week than in six months with a psychoanalyst.   *Adlai Stevenson II*

1 Still in Trouble

I am dying as I have lived – beyond my means. – *Oscar Levant*

2 Your Enemies

Forgive your enemies, but don't forget their names.

John F. Kennedy

3 No Yes Men

I don't want any yes-men around me. I want everybody to tell me the truth even if it costs them their jobs.   *Samuel Goldwyn*

4 A Short Distance

History is the short trudge from Adam to atom.

‘

1 The Defence

Dr. Robert J. Oppenheimer, who supervised the creation of the first atomic bomb, appeared before a US congressional committee. They enquired of him if there was any defence against the weapon.

‘Certainly,’ the great physicist replied.

‘And that is −’

Dr Oppenheimer looked over the hushed, expectant audience and said softly: ‘Peace.’   *Christian Science Monitor*

2 Seven Deadly Sins

E. Stanley Jones, a one-time American missionary, statesman and author-lecturer, formulated what he termed seven deadly sins: ‘Politics without principle; wealth without work; pleasure without conscience; knowledge without character; business without morality; science without humanity; and worship without sacrifice.’

3 Our Most Powerful Weapon

Democracy’s most powerful weapon is not a gun, tank or bomb. It is faith − faith in brotherhood and in the dignity of men under God.
Harry S. Truman

4 What We Lose

Living in rented apartments, jamming roads and subways, punching time clocks, cramming the minds of children with technical knowledge, modern man sacrifices health of body and freedom of spirit to the scientific idol of his time. On its altar go the smell of earth, the feel of wind and weather, warmth of friendship, understanding of children, even the contemplation of God; all these are given over to a metallic existence.   *Charles A. Lindbergh*

5 Tact

Charles Schwab, a distinguished American industrialist, knew how to deal with his workers. One day as he walked through a factory he saw three men smoking where they shouldn’t have been. He did not reprimand them. He simply reached in his pocket, took out three cigars and said, ‘Boys, have a cigar on me − but I should appreciate it if you would not smoke it here during working hours.’

’

1 Disagree

Business is built by men who care enough to disagree, fight it out to the finish, get the facts. When two men always agree, one of them is unnecessary. *William Wrigley, Jr.*

2 Still Around

'I'd like to be around when I'm 100 and playing in a show being staged on the moon.' *Bob Hope*

3 Our Salvation

Our salvation, and our only salvation, lies in controlling the arm of Western science by the mind of a Western philosophy guided by God's eternal truths. *Charles A. Lindbergh*

4 Self-Pity

Self-pity is our worst enemy and if we yield to it, we can never do anything wise in the world. *Helen Keller*

5 Couldn't Deny It

When a lawyer characterized Frank Lloyd Wright as America's greatest architect, Wright confessed to his wife that he could not deny it because he was under oath.

6 Don't Try It

The most dangerous thing in the world is to leap a chasm in two jumps. *David Lloyd George*

7 Make No Little Plans

Make no little plans; they have no magic to stir men's blood and probably themselves will not be realized. Make big plans; aim high in hope and work, remembering that a noble, logical diagram once recorded will never die, but long after we are gone will be a living thing, asserting itself with ever-growing insistency.

Daniel Hudson Burnham, architect

‘

1 The Spirit and Mind of Man

We know that there is no true and lasting cure for world tensions in guns and bombs. We know that only the spirit and mind of man, dedicated to justice and right, can, in the long term, enable us to live in the confident tranquillity that should be every man's heritage.

Dwight D. Eisenhower

2 Difficult Secret to Keep

The most difficult secret for a man to keep is his own opinion of himself.   *Marcel Pagnol*

3 His Monument

Sir Christopher Wren, architect of St Paul's Cathedral, had the following inscription in Latin carved above one of the entrances: 'If you seek my monument, look around you.'

4 Way Back in 1784

On 16 January, 1784, Benjamin Franklin foresaw the danger of 'parachute troops'. He witnessed successful balloon flights over the city of Paris, and on that date he wrote to a friend in France: 'It appears, as you observe, to be a discovery of great importance and what may possibly give a new turn to human affairs.... Five thousand balloons, capable of raising two men each, could not cost more than five ships of the line, and where is the prince who can afford so to cover his country with troops for its defence, as that ten thousand men descending from the clouds might not in many places do an infinite deal of mischief, before a force could be brought together to repel them?'

5 The Guidance We Need

Belief in God and in immortality gives us the moral strength and the ethical guidance we need for virtually every action in our daily lives.

Wernher von Braun ’

' 1 Opportunity Tried to Knock

They say opportunity knocks once, but only once. Here are a few instances when her knock was not heard.

In 1911 a plumber submitted to the War Office a design for a tank – a then unknown military device. Across the drawing, in red ink, was written the official comment: 'This man is mad.'

One day a stranger approached the famous author Mark Twain with a request for $500 in return for a half interest in his invention. Twain who had been caught like this several times before, refused flatly. But out of courtesy he asked the stranger his name. 'Bell,' the man replied, as he turned away, 'Alexander Graham Bell.'

It wasn't a stranger who approached Sir Arthur Conan Doyle, the creator of Sherlock Holmes. A young actor playing in one of the writer's productions suggested that they divide their incomes with each other for the rest of their lives. Conan Doyle laughed heartily. 'Charlie Chaplin,' he said, 'if I didn't know you were joking, I'd have you fired for such audacity.'

2 Dale Carnegie's Six Rules for Winning Friends

1. Be genuinely interested in other people.
2. Smile. A man without a smiling face must not open a shop.
3. Remember that a man's name is to him the sweetest and most important sound in the language.
4. Be a good listener. Encourage others to talk about themselves. Many persons call a doctor when all they want is an audience.
5. Talk in terms of the other man's interest.
6. Make the other person feel important – and do it with sincerity.

' 1 Herbert Hoover's Bill of Rights for Boys

1. Like everybody else, a boy has a right to the pursuit of happiness.
2. He has the right to play so that he may stretch his imagination and prove his prowess and skill.
3. He has the right to the constructive joys of adventure and the thrills that are a part of an open life.
4. He has a right to affection and friendship.
5. He has a right to the sense of security in belonging to some group.
6. He has a right to health protection that will make him an inch taller than his dad.
7. He has a right to the education and training that will amplify his own natural bents, and fit him into a job.
8. And I would add another right – the right to accept the obligations of citizenship in a democracy – perhaps the greatest right a boy, or anyone else, can have.

2 Warnings

Some two thousand years ago Plutarch warned: 'The real destroyer of the liberties of people is he who spreads among them bounties, donations, and benefits.'

An old French peasant made this sad observation after the collapse of France early in World War II (France was burdened with social subsidies): 'My country fell because we had come to consider France a cow to be milked – not a watchdog to feed.'

3 Coolidge Saved Time

When Calvin Coolidge was President of the USA, he saw dozens of people each day. Most had complaints of one kind or another. A visiting state governor once told the President that he did not understand how he could see so many people in the space of a few hours. 'Why, you are finished with them by dinner time,' the governor remarked, 'while I'm often at my desk until midnight.'

'Yes,' said Coolidge, 'but you talk back.' '

1 War

I confess without shame that I am tired and sick of the war. Its glory is all moonshine. Even victory the most brilliant is over dead and mangled bodies, the anguish and lamentation of distant families crying to me for missing sons, husbands, and fathers. It is only those who have not heard the shrieks and groans of the wounded and lacerated, that clamor for more blood, more vengance, more desolation.

William Tecumseh Sherman, American Civil War general

2 No Little Thing

Mark Twain told of the time his little girl broke her doll, and he attempted to quiet her sobbing by making light of the incident. 'You shouldn't cry over a little thing like that.'

But she, looking up through her tears, asked: 'Daddy, what is a little thing?' and he was unable to answer, for her broken doll was as important to her as a kingdom to a monarch.

3 More to Life

There is more to life than increasing its speed.   *Mahatma Gandhi*

4 Laughter

Laughter is the shortest distance between two people.

Victor Borge

5 Always in Search

The Good Shepherd is always in search of the lost sheep.

Bishop Fulton J. Sheen

6 Heredity

Heredity is an omnibus in which all our ancestors ride, and every now and then one of them puts his head out and embarrasses us.

Oliver Wendell Holmes

' ## 1 His Philosophy of Life

The best thing to give to your enemy is forgiveness; to an opponent, tolerance; to a friend, your heart; to your child, a good example; to a father, deference; to your mother, conduct that will make her proud of you; to yourself, respect; to all men, charity.

Arthur James Balfour

2 The Human Race

Such is the human race. Often it does seem such a pity that Noah . . . didn't miss the boat. *Mark Twain*

3 Vice or Virtue

Extremism in the defense of liberty is no vice. . . . Moderation in the pursuit of justice is no virtue. *Barry Goldwater*

4 A Short Memory

Nothing is so admirable in politics as a short memory.

John Kenneth Galbraith

5 The Same All Over

Politicians are the same all over. They promise to build a bridge even where there is no river. *Nikita Khrushchev*

6 Innocent Employment

There are few ways in which a man can be more innocently employed than in getting money. *Dr Samuel Johnson*

7 Irish: Eloquent

My one claim to originality among Irishmen is that I have never made a speech. *George Moore*

'

1 It's Difficult

The hardest job kids face today is learning good manners without seeing any.   *Fred Astaire*

2 His Concern

I don't know who my grandfather was; I am much more concerned to know what his grandson will be.   *Abraham Lincoln*

3 Napoleon's Philosophy

The word 'impossible' is not in my dictionary.

Napoleon Bonaparte

4 Conceited

He is a self-made man and worships his creator.

John Bright, referring to Disraeli

5 Whose Fault

Now when I bore people at a party they think it's their fault.

Henry Kissinger

6 Diplomacy

Franz Liszt, no less a diplomat than a musician, had a stock reply for young women who demanded unmerited praise of their singing.

'Maestro,' a young woman would enquire, 'do you think I have a good voice?'

'Ah, my dear young lady,' Lizst would reply with the utmost sincerity, ' "good" is not the word to describe it!'

'

6

Thoughtful comments on important subjects

1 Crowds Never

Individuals are occasionally guided by reason, crowds never.

Dean W. R. Inge

2 A Good Rule

When in doubt, tell the truth. *Mark Twain*

3 No Successful Liar

No man has a memory long enough to be a successful liar.

Abraham Lincoln

4 When Truth Is Violated

Truth is not only violated by falsehood; it may be equally outraged by silence.   *Henry Frederic Amiel*

5 The Strongest Argument

The truth is always the strongest argument.   *Sophocles*

‘ 1 The Measure of a Person

The measure of a person is not the number of people who serve him, but the number of people he serves.

2 Greatness

The great man is to be the servant of mankind, not they of him.

3 Serving Others

I don't know what your destiny will be, but one thing I know, the only ones among you who will be really happy are those who have sought and found how to serve. *Albert Schweitzer*

4 Take Time to Decide

Set aside a little time once a year, at least, to decide where you are going, what are your priorities, ambitions, aspirations. Not just in your business alone, but also in the personal things – your own free evenings, your own feelings of status and worthwhileness in life, and your own dignity, your own integrity, your family.

William C. Menninger

5 An Open Heart

There is dew in one flower and not in another, because one opens its cup and takes it in, while the other closes itself, and the dewdrops run off. God rains his goodness and mercy as widespread as the dew, and if we lack them, it is because we will not open our hearts to receive them. *Henry Ward Beecher*

6 How to Live

But when thou makest a feast, call the poor, the maimed, the lame, the blind: and thou shalt be blessed. *Luke 14:13*

7 Democracy

Democracy means not 'I am as good as you are,' but 'You are as good as I am.' *Theodore Parker* ’

'

1 The First Duty

The first duty toward children is to make them happy. If you have not made them happy, you have wronged them; no other good they may get can make up for that.   *Charles Buxton*

2 What a Father Can Do

The most important thing a father can do for his children is to demonstrate his love and admiration for their mother.

3 The Purpose of Education

The purpose of education is to transmit the culture of a society to its young. In accomplishing this, it is hoped that the individual will be armed with knowledge, strength of judgement and moral virtues, as well as the ability to make a living, and in the process, preserve the heritage of the nation and the achievements of previous generations.

4 Father to Son

Advice from a father to his son: 'My boy, treat everybody with politeness, even those who are rude to you. For remember that you show courtesy to others not because *they* are gentlemen, but because *you* are one.'

5 What Everyone Likes to Be Told

Never be sparing with words of appreciation, especially when they are deserved by those around us. Everyone likes to be told that they are admired, respected, appreciated and even liked.

6 Character

A man's character is the reality of himself. His reputation is the opinion others have formed of him. Character is in him; reputation is from other people – that is the substance, this is the shadow.

7 Reputation and Character

A person's reputation is precious, but a person's character is priceless.

'

❛ 1 What He Believed

I believe in the sacredness of a promise, that a man's word should be as good as his bond; that character – not wealth or power or position – is of supreme worth. *John D. Rockefeller, Jr*

2 He Likes Autumn

I like spring, but it is too young. I like summer, but it is too proud. So I like best of all autumn, because its leaves are a little yellow, its tone mellower, its colours richer, and it is tinged a little with sorrow....Its golden richness speaks not of the innocence of spring, nor of the power of summer, but of the mellowness and kindly wisdom of approaching age. It knows the limitations of life and is content.

3 Few Have Imagination

The opportunities of man are limited by only his imagination. But so few have imagination that there are ten thousand fiddlers to one composer.

4 Lincoln's Conviction

I can see how it might be possible for a man to look down upon the earth and be an atheist, but I cannot conceive how he could look up into the heavens and say there is no God. *Abraham Lincoln*

5 The Shortcomings of Others

Too many of us become enraged because we have to bear the shortcomings of others. We should remember that not one of us is perfect, and that others see our defects as obviously as we see theirs. We forget too often to look at ourselves through the eyes of our friends. Let us, therefore, bear the shortcomings of each other for the ultimate benefit of everyone. *Abraham Lincoln*

6 New Ideas

If you want to succeed you should strike out on new paths rather than travel the worn paths of accepted success.

John D. Rockefeller ❜

' **1 Man Will Prevail**

I believe that man will not merely endure, he will prevail . . . because he has a soul, a spirit capable of compassion and sacrifice and endurance.   *William Faulkner*

2 Not Easy

A child should always say what's true
And speak when he is spoken to,
And behave mannerly at table;
At least as far as he is able.   *Robert Louis Stevenson*

3 Constant Trials

We are always in the forge, or on the anvil; by trials God is shaping us for higher things.

4 Circumstances

Man is not the creature of circumstance; circumstances are the creatures of man.   *Benjamin Disraeli*

5 Using Circumstances

The ideal man bears the accidents of life with dignity and grace, making the best of circumstances.   *Aristotle*

'

‘
1 The Years Teach One

The years teach much which the days never know.

Ralph Waldo Emerson

2 Modesty in Everyone

In his private heart no man much respects himself.   *Mark Twain*

3 Dreams

We grow by dreams. All big men are dreamers. They see things in the soft haze of a spring day, or in the red fire of a long winter's evening. Some of us let these great dreams die, but others nourish and protect them, nurse them through bad days till they bring them to the light which comes always to those who sincerely hope that their dreams will come true.   *Woodrow Wilson*

4 His View of Life

The longer I live, the more beautiful life becomes.

Frank Lloyd Wright

5 The Greatest Victory

Self-conquest is the greatest of all victories.   *Plato*

6 Mother

A man takes counsel with his wife; he obeys his mother. Let France have good mothers and she will have good sons.

Napoleon Bonaparte

A mother is not to lean on but to make leaning unnecessary.

Dorothy Fisher

All that I am or hope to be I owe to my angel mother.

Abraham Lincoln ’

' **1 What the Cynic Sees**

The cynic is one who never sees a good quality in a man, and never fails to see a bad one. He is the human owl, vigilant in darkness and blind to light, mousing for vermin, and never seeing noble game. The cynic puts all human actions into two classes – openly bad and secretly bad.   *Henry Ward Beecher*

2 A Big Difference

You'll never find the line
'Money is the root of all evil'
in the Bible. But you will find that it states,
'Love of money is the root of all evil.'
There's a big difference.

3 Determination

A determined soul will do more with a rusty monkey wrench than a loafer will accomplish with all the tools in a machine shop.

4 What Would You Have If You Reached Your Goal?

In a little country community a farmer had a dog who spent part of his time sitting by the side of the main road waiting for big lorries. When the dog saw a large lorry come around the corner, he would get ready, and as the lorry passed him he would rush out after it down the road, barking and doing his best to overtake it.

One day the farmer's neighbour said, 'Sam, do you think that dog of yours is ever going to catch a lorry?'

'Well, Bill,' Sam replied, 'That isn't what worries me. What worries me is what he would do if he caught one!'

Many of us in life are like that dog. We give our lives pursuing goals that have little value even if we reach them. Sometimes it pays to stop and ask whether we have objectives worth pursuing.

5 Most Valuable

The most valuable thing I have learned from life is to regret nothing.   *Somerset Maugham*   '

1 Making the Best of It

There are no circumstances, however unfortunate, that clever people do not extract some advantage from.

2 Learning from Failure

Failure is instructive. The person who really thinks learns quite as much from his failures as from his successes.   *John Dewey*

3 When We Are Wrong

A man should never be ashamed to own he has been in the wrong, which is but saying in other words, that he is wiser today than he was yesterday.   *Alexander Pope*

4 Problems

Problems are opportunities and there are a lot of them around.

5 Trouble

Opportunity wears many disguises, including trouble.

6 Plausible and Wrong

There is always an easy solution to every human problem – neat, plausible and wrong.

7 The Present Hour

One of the illusions of life is that the present hour is not the critical, decisive hour. Write it on your heart that every day is the best day of the year. He only is rich who owns the day, and no one owns the day who allows it to be invaded with worry, fret and anxiety. Finish every day, and be done with it. You have done what you could.
Ralph Waldo Emerson

8 Writing Is Easy

Writing is easy. All you do is stare at a blank sheet of paper until drops of blood form on your forehead.   *Gene Fowler*

1 The Best Foreign Policy

Honesty is also the best foreign policy.

2 Thinking

Few people think more than two or three times a year. I have made an international reputation for myself by thinking once or twice a week. *George Bernard Shaw*

3 The Misfortune

No one is exempt from talking nonsense; the misfortune is to do it solemnly. *Michel de Montaigne*

4 Giving

We should give as we would receive, cheerfully, quickly and without hesitation, for there is no grace in a benefit that sticks to the fingers. *Seneca*

5 You Gain

What is done for another is done for oneself. *Paulus*

6 Three Things Necessary

Three things are necessary for the salvation of man: to know what he ought to believe, to know what he ought to desire, and to know what he ought to do. *St Thomas Aquinas*

7 Your Viewpoint

We think too small. Like the frog at the bottom of the well. He thinks the sky is only as big as the top of the well. If he surfaced, he would have an entirely different view. *Mao Tse-Tung*

'

1 Still Learning

I am still learning.   *Michelangelo*

2 Reality

One of the criteria of emotional maturity is having the ability to deal constructively with reality.

3 For Others

Everyone has a code of ethics for everyone.

'

1 Just Forget

Be a good forgetter. Forget the things that are behind; forget injuries, slights, unkind words; be too big too be hurt; be too great to be unkind; be too busy to quarrel; too wise to engage in unseemly gossip; too strong to permit little annoyances to turn you from life's big road; too clean to stain your character with any kind of muckraking.   *Good Reading*

2 Many of Us Do

Don't make the mistake of letting yesterday use up too much of today.

3 Moments of Prayer

Certain thoughts are prayers. There are moments when, whatever be the attitude of the body, the soul is on its knees.   *Victor Hugo*

4 Only Once

I expect to pass through this world but once. Any good, therefore, that I can do, or any kindness that I can show to any fellow creature, let me do it now. Let me not defer or neglect it, for I shall not pass this way again.   *Stephen Grellet*

5 Free to Argue

It is not necessary to understand things in order to argue about them.   *Pierre Augustin de Beaumarchais*

6 What Adversity Does

Adversity reminds men of religion.   *Livy*

7 Most of Us

The mass of men lead lives of quiet desperation.

Henry David Thoreau

1 From the Heart

In friendship we find nothing false or insincere; everything is straightforward and springs from the heart.   *Cicero*

2 Your Character

A man never discloses his own character so clearly as when he describes another's.   *Jean Paul Richter*

3 A Nuisance

It is a nuisance that knowledge can only be acquired by hard work. *Somerset Maugham*

4 Life

To lengthen thy life, lessen thy meals.   *Benjamin Franklin*

5 Ideas

For an idea that does not at first seem insane, there is no hope.
Albert Einstein

6 A Good Reputation

The way to gain a good reputation is to endeavour to be what you desire to appear.   *Socrates*

7 Atomic Age

The Atomic Age is here to stay − but are we?

8 The Greatest Medicine

Me retire? I'd die before I'd give up hearing an audience laugh. It's the greatest tonic, the greatest medicine, in the world.   *Bob Hope*

9 The Reason

Few men are lacking in capacity, but they fail because they are lacking in application.

1 A Great Legacy

Books are the legacies that a great genius leaves to mankind, which are delivered down from generation to generation, as presents to the posterity of those who are yet unborn.   *Joseph Addison*

2 The Meaning of Democracy

Democracy substitutes election by the incompetent many for appointment by the corrupt few.   *George Bernard Shaw*

3 Old Age

The harvest of old age is the memory and rich store of blessings laid up in earlier life.   *Cicero*

4 Beauty

When the candles are out all women are fair.   *Plutarch*

5 The Calibre of a Person

The calibre of a person is to be found in the ability to meet disappointment and be enriched rather than embittered by it.

6 Management

Management by objectives works if you know the objectives. Ninety per cent of the time you don't.

7 The Real Test

Profitability is the sovereign criterion of the enterprise.

8 What the Bible Teaches

The scriptures teach us the best way of living, the noblest way of suffering, and the most comfortable way of dying.   *John Flavel*

' 1 The Way to a Man's Heart

The royal road to a man's heart is to talk to him about the things he treasures most.   *Dale Carnegie*

2 Naturally

It is one of the most beautiful compensations of life that no man can sincerely try to help another without helping himself.

William Shakespeare

3 Keeps Coming Back

Kindness is a hard thing to give away. It keeps coming back to the giver.

4 How to Forget Troubles

A good way to forget your troubles is to help others out of theirs.

5 Delay

The greatest remedy for anger is delay.   *Seneca*

6 How Short Life Is

When thou art above measure angry, bethink thee how momentary is man's life.   *Marcus Aurelius*

7 Where God Is Found

God is found in two places; one of his dwellings is Heaven, and the other is in a meek and thankful heart.

8 Money

Light purse, heavy heart.   *Benjamin Franklin*

9 What Art Does

Without art, the crudeness of reality would make the world unbearable.   *George Bernard Shaw*   '

1 God's Revelation

The Bible is God's revelation to man, his guide, his light.
Alfred Armand Montapert

2 Time Is Flying

Gather ye rose-buds while ye may,
Old Time is still a-flying:
And this same flower that smiles today,
Tomorrow will be dying.   *Robert Herrick*

3 Ability

Natural ability without education has more often raised a man to
glory and virtue than education without natural ability.   *Cicero*

4 Loving One's Neighbour

It is easier to love humanity as a whole than to love one's neighbour.

5 When We Believe

We are inclined to believe those we do not know, because they have
never deceived us.   *Samuel Johnson*

6 Progress

To be conscious that you are ignorant is a great step towards
knowledge.

7 The Problem

Most of God's troubles with labourers in his vineyard can be traced
to absenteeism.   *The Protestant Voice*

8 A Hard Teacher

Experience is a hard teacher because she gives the test first, the
lesson afterwards.

‘ **1 Conceit**

Conceit is a closer companion of ignorance than of learning.

2 Talent and Character

Talent is built in solitude; character in the stream of the world.

Goethe

3 Everything But

Money can buy you everything but happiness and pay your fare to every place but heaven.

,

1 The Real Test

There is no better test for a man's ultimate integrity than his behaviour when he is wrong.

2 Why Is It?

Why is it in a civilized nation that happiness and intelligence are so seldom found together?

3 Greatest Joy

An old Chinese philosopher was asked what was the greatest joy he had found in life. 'A child,' he said, 'going down the road singing after asking me the way.'

4 It Isn't Easy

To be poor without being resentful is difficult; to be rich without being arrogant is even harder.

5 What We Need to Learn

In modern times, man has learned how to split the atom and build planes that conquer space and distance and bring people the world over within hours and minutes of each other; yet man has not been able to find a formula that enables men of different races, cultures, personalities and religions to live together amicably.

6 Ominous Sounds

In world affairs, nothing sounds so ominous as the rumbling of empty stomachs.

7 Silence May Be Wisdom

Silence at the proper season is wisdom, and better than any speech.

Plutarch

1 What We Value

What men value in this world is not rights but privileges.

H. L. Mencken

2 Rights and Obligations

With every civil right there has to be a corresponding civil obligation. – *Edison Haines*

3 Youth in Old Age

Old age is not a disease. Because a person is old, he is not inadequate. There is youth in old age, and beauty too, if we only have the eyes to see.

4 Your Life

Every life is a work of art, shaped by the person who lives it.

5 Same Value

The conservative who resists change is as valuable as the radical who proposes it.   *Will and Ariel Durant*

6 Greatness

It takes a great man to make a good listener.   *Sir Arthur Helps*

7 Our Age

Perfection of means and confusion of ends seem to characterize our age.   *Albert Einstein*

8 Costs Too Much

Laughter costs too much if it is purchased by the sacrifice of decency.

'

1 No Less Important

The prayers a person lives on his feet are no less important than those he says on his knees.

2 An Important Voice

What a father says to his children is not heard by the world, but it will be heard by posterity.

3 The Power of Example

There is a transcendent power in example. We reform others unconsciously, when we walk uprightly.

4 The Importance of the Family

No nation can be destroyed while it possesses a good home life.

5 Famous Inscriptions

Over one of the doors of Milan Cathedral is a cross beneath which are the words: 'All that troubles is but for a moment.' Under the great central entrance in the main aisle is the inscription: 'That only is important which is eternal.'

'

1 Government

An empty stomach is not a good political adviser.   *Albert Einstein*

2 Aims

The great thing in this world is not so much where we are, but in what direction we are going.   *Oliver Wendell Holmes*

3 Democracy

Democracy is based on the conviction that there are extraordinary possibilities in ordinary people.   *Harry Emerson Fosdick*

4 Livelihood

He that hath a trade, hath an estate. He that hath a calling, hath an office of profit and honour.   *Benjamin Franklin*

5 True Wisdom

The wise know too well their own weakness to assume infallibility; and he who knows most, knows how little he knows.

Thomas Jefferson

6 Goals

To be what we are and to become what we are capable of becoming, is the only end of life.   *Robert Louis Stevenson*

7 Habit

Habit is a cable; we weave a thread of it each day, and at last we cannot break it.   *Horace Mann*

8 What Difficulties Do

If there were no difficulties, there would be no triumphs.

1 The Difference

An optimist sees an opportunity in every calamity; a pessimist sees a calamity in every opportunity.　*Winston Churchill*

2 Never Lost

No opportunity is ever lost; someone else picks up those you miss.

3 Hope

There has always been a sunrise after a sunset.

4 Expect Changes in Your Friends

The only man who behaved sensibly was my tailor; he took my measure anew every time he saw me, whilst all the rest went on with their old measurements and expected them to fit me.

George Bernard Shaw

5 To Be Contented

It is right to be contented with what we have, never with what we are.　*Sir James Mackintosh*

6 Selfishness

Selfishness is the great unknown sin. No selfish person ever thought himself selfish.

7 A Prayer

Lord, make me an instrument of Thy Peace. Where there is hatred, let me sow love, where there is injury, pardon; whence there is doubt, faith; where there is despair, hope; where there is darkness, light; and where there is sickness, joy. O Divine Master, grant that I may not so much seek to be consoled as to console; to be understood as to understand; to be loved as to love; for it is in giving that we receive; it is in pardoning that we are pardoned; and it is in dying that we are born to eternal life.　*St Francis of Assisi*

1 Common Weakness

Man's most pitiful weakness is his desire to get something for nothing.

2 Luxury Loving

Man is a luxury-loving animal. His greatest exertions are made in pursuit not of necessities but of superfluities.   *Eric Hoffer*

3 Wanting to Win

Winning isn't everything − but wanting to win is.

Vince Lombardi

4 Experience

Experience is not what happens to a man. It is what a man does with what happens to him.   *Aldous Huxley*

5 What He Believes

For my part I believe in the forgiveness of sin and the redemption of ignorance.   *Adlai Stevenson*

' 1 Why Nations Decline and Fall

In 1788 Edward Gibbon set forth in his famous book *Decline and Fall of the Roman Empire* five basic reasons why that great civilization withered and died.

1. The undermining of the dignity and sanctity of the home, which is the basis for human society.
2. Higher and higher taxes: the spending of public money for free bread and circuses for the populace.
3. The mad craze for pleasure, with sports and plays becoming more exciting, more brutal and more immoral.
4. The building of great armaments when the real enemy was within – decay of individual responsibility.
5. The decay of religion, whose leaders lost touch with life and their power to guide.

2 The Right Way to Live

Constantly speak the truth, boldly rebuke vice, and patiently suffer for the truth's sake.   *Book of Common Prayer*

3 Reading Enriches

It is not true that we have only one life to live; if we can read, we can live as many more lives and as many kinds as we wish.

S. I. Hayakawa

4 The Value of Time

There is nothing that we can properly call our own but our time, and yet everybody fools us out of it who has a mind to do it. If a man borrows a paltry sum of money, there must needs be bonds and securities. But he who has my time thinks he owes me nothing for it, though it be a debt that gratitude itself can never repay.

Seneca

5 Self-Taught

Very few men are wise by their own counsel, or learned by their own teaching; for he that was only taught by himself had a fool to his master.   *Ben Jonson*

‘

1 One Thing Remains

All the good maxims have been written. It only remains to put them into practice. *Blaise Pascal*

2 Common Sense

One of the grave maladies of our time is the way sophistication seems to be valued above common sense. Words cease to have the plain meaning assigned to them and become wildly elastic. The manipulation of an idea seems to be more important than the integrity of an idea.

3 One Qualification

Sir Winston Churchill, asked what qualifications were essential for a politician, replied: 'The ability to foretell what will happen tomorrow, next month and next year – and to explain afterwards why it didn't happen.'

4 The Biggest Mistake

The biggest mistake is the fear that you will make one.

5 It's Disguised

Only a comparative few recognize opportunity because it is disguised as hard work.

6 Our Task

Our task now is not to fix the blame for the past, but to fix the course for the future. *John F. Kennedy*

’

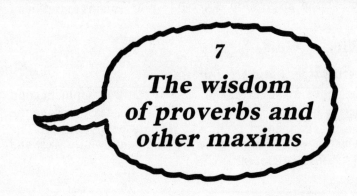

7
The wisdom of proverbs and other maxims

1 Real Loss

He that loses his honesty has nothing else to lose.

2 The Darkest Hour

The darkest hour is just before dawn.

3 Idleness

Idle people have the least leisure.

4 Honour Thy Father

He that honoureth his father shall have a long life.

5 Finding Fault

A father loves his children in hating their faults.

French proverb

1 Concentration

Ninety per cent of inspiration is perspiration.

2 Objectivity

Hear the other side. *Latin proverb*

3 Doing Well

Thinking well is wise; planning well, wiser; doing well, wisest and best of all.   *Persian proverb*

4 All Good Things Are Yours

Fear less, hope more;
Eat less, chew more;
Whine less, breathe more;
Talk less, say more;
Hate less, love more;
And all good things are yours.   *Swedish proverb*

5 Persistence

Little drops of water wear down big stones.   *Russian proverb*

6 Your Parents

Next to God, thy parents.   *William Penn*

7 Repose

Only in the grave is there rest.   *Yiddish proverb*

8 Happiness in Moderation

Happiness is a halfway station between too little and too much.

9 The Key

A golden key opens all doors.   *Yiddish proverb*

1 Character

Men show their characters in what they think laughable.   *Goethe*

2 Liar

A liar believes no one.   *Yiddish proverb*

3 Humility

Life is a long lesson in humility.   *James Barrie*

4 Shortness of Days

As for man, his days are as grass.   *Psalm 103:15*

5 What Adversity Does

Adversity introduces a man to himself.

6 Old Error

An old error is always more popular than a new truth.
German proverb

7 Half Truth

A half truth is a whole lie.   *Yiddish proverb*

8 Typical of Vermont

Don't talk unless you can improve on silence.   *Vermont proverb*

9 Don't Call Names

No call alligator long mouth till you pass him.   *Jamaican proverb*

10 Generosity

He who gives to me teaches me to give.   *Danish proverb*

1 Praise

Praise the wise man behind his back, but a woman to her face.
Welsh proverb

2 Debt of Kindness

One can pay back the loan of gold, but one dies forever in debt to those who are kind.   *Malayan proverb*

3 Too Late

Advice comes too late when a thing is done.

4 Carried Away

Fury and anger carry the mind away.   *Virgil*

5 Argument

In a heated argument we are apt to lose sight of the truth.
Latin proverb

6 Temptation

The bait hides the hook.

7 Shorter Is Better

It is better to be brief than tedious.   *Shakespeare*

8 Strength

God gives the shoulder according to the burden.
German proverb

9 The Victor

He is twice a conqueror, who can restrain himself in the hour of victory.   *Latin proverb*

'

1 Conscience

He who has no conscience has nothing. *French proverb*

2 Contentment

The best of blessings – a contented mind. *Latin proverb*

3 Courtesy

Courtesy costs nothing.

4 Descent

Every beggar is descended from some king, and every king from some beggar.

'

' **1 Immortality**

God created man to be immortal.   *Apocrypha*

2 Opportunity

Through indecision, opportunity is often lost.   *Latin proverb*

3 Injury

The worthy man forgets past injuries.   *Greek proverb*

4 No Easy Way

There is no royal road to learning.   *Euclid*

5 Judgment

Life is not measured by the time we live.

6 Life and Death

Life is nearer every day to death.   *Latin proverb*

7 Good Deed

The reward for a good deed is to have done it.

8 Humility

Cap in hand never did anyone harm.   *Italian proverb*

9 Typically English

The first of all English games is making money.   *John Ruskin*

10 The Value of Proverbs

A proverb is one man's wit and all men's wisdom.
Lord John Russell '

1 Bacon Comments on Proverbs

The genius, wit and spirit of a nation are discovered in its proverbs.

Francis Bacon

2 Choices

It is better to walk than run;
It is better to stand than to walk;
It is better to sit than to stand;
It is better to lie than to sit.   *Hindu proverb*

3 Inevitable

Every silver lining has a cloud.

4 The Reason for Mothers

God could not be everywhere and therefore he made mothers.

Jewish proverb

5 The Mob

The mob has many heads but no brains.

English proverb, seventeenth century

6 Learned Folly

Natural folly is bad enough, but learned folly is intolerable.

English proverb, eighteenth century

7 Three Classes

All mankind is divided into three classes: those that are immovable, those that are movable, and those that move.

Arabian proverb

8 No Doubts

Who knows nothing doubts nothing.   *French proverb*

1 Untimely

Economy is too late at the bottom of the purse.   *Latin proverb*

2 Results

In everything consider the end.   *French proverb*

3 An Enemy

Man is his own worst enemy.   *Latin proverb*

4 Truth

No epigram contains the whole truth.

5 Virtue

We are all born equal, and distinguished alone by virtue.

Latin proverb

6 Failure

He who never fails will never grow rich.

7 Faith

I have kept the faith.   *New Testament, II Timothy*

8 Fall

All things that rise will fall.   *Latin proverb*

9 Fame

The temple of fame stands upon the grave.

10 Chatter

Fools cannot hold their tongues.   *Chaucer*

1 A Fool

None is a fool always, everyone sometimes.

2 Freedom

To be free is to live under a government by law.

3 Tolerance

A friend should bear his friend's infirmities.   *Shakespeare*

4 No Gossip

He is a good friend that speaks well of me behind my back.

5 Be Careful of Friends

A friend must not be wounded, even in jest.   *Latin proverb*

6 Friendship

The only way to have a friend is to be one.

7 When Friendship Counts

Be more ready to visit a friend in adversity than in prosperity.
Greek proverb

8 Risk

To make any gain some outlay is necessary. *Dutch proverb*

9 Wealth

Gold goes in at any gate, except Heaven's.

10 Example

The good man makes others good.   *Greek proverb*

1 Foolishness

Better be a coward than foolhardy.   *French proverb*

2 Mortality

In the midst of life we are in death.   *Book of Common Prayer*

3 Death

Death spares neither pope nor beggar.   *Italian proverb*

4 Maturity

Reason does not come before years.   *German proverb*

5 Permanence

Nothing can be lasting when reason does not rule.   *Latin proverb*

6 Reform

Every reform movement has a lunatic fringe.   *Theodore Roosevelt*

1 Equality of Death

For who's a prince or beggar in the grave?   *Thomas Otway*

2 Hatred

Hatred is self-punishment.

3 Health

Health is not valued till sickness comes.

4 Humility

Humility often gains more than pride.   *Italian proverb*

5 Mercy

Mercy surpasses justice.   *Chaucer*

6 Trifles

Light minds are pleased with trifles.   *Latin proverb*

7 Mind

The mind is the man.   *Latin proverb*

8 Misfortune

Misfortune does not always come to injure.   *Italian proverb*

9 Learn from Others' Mistakes

Learn to see in another's misfortune the ills which you should avoid.
Latin proverb

10 Moderation

True happiness springs from moderation.   *German proverb*

‘

1 Mortality

Remember that thou art mortal.   *Greek proverb*

2 Need

Necessity breaks iron.

3 Stubborn

The foolish and the dead alone never change their opinions.

4 Manners

One never loses anything by politeness.

5 Position

He sits not sure that sits too high.

6 Distinction

If you are poor, distinguish yourself by your virtues; if rich, by your good deeds.   *French proverb*

7 Praise

One has only to die to be praised.   *German proverb*

8 Prayer

Prayer is a wish turned heavenward.

9 Prejudice

It is never too late to give up our prejudices.

Henry David Thoreau

10 Luxury

What you do not need is dear at a farthing.   *Latin proverb*

’

1 Pride

The proud hate pride – in others.

2 Faults

Pride is the mask of one's own faults.   *Hebrew proverb*

3 Procrastination

By and by never comes.   *Latin proverb*

4 Prosperity

In prosperity, caution; in adversity, patience.

5 Faith

God provides for him that trusteth.

6 Suffering

Man's inhumanity to man makes countless thousands mourn.
Robert Burns

7 Marriage

It is not marriage that fails; it is people that fail.

8 Prosperity

We are corrupted by prosperity.   *Tacitus*

9 Most Difficult

The most difficult thing of all, to keep quiet and listen.
Aulus Gellius

10 Fools

Fools are wise until they speak.   *Randle Cotgrave*

'

1 Man

Man is a tool-using animal.   *Thomas Carlyle*

2 Modesty

Modesty is the only sure bait when you angle for praise.
Lord Chesterfield

3 Silence

He knew the precise psychological moment to say nothing.
Oscar Wilde

4 Cheerfulness

A merry heart maketh a cheerful countenance.   *Proverbs 15:13*

5 A Cure

Money cures melancholy.   *John Ray*

6 Time

Nothing is ours except time.   *Seneca*

7 Time Flows On

Time is a river of passing events, aye, a rushing torrent.
Marcus Aurelius

8 Eternity

Time is the image of eternity.   *Plato*

9 Metropolis

A great city, a great solitude.

'

1 Cleverness

Cleverness is not wisdom. *Euripides*

2 To Cure Anger

When angry, count to a hundred.

3 The Devil's Delight

To curse is to pray to the Devil. *German proverb*

4 Compliments

I much prefer a compliment, insincere or not, to sincere criticism.
Plautus

5 Partly Sincere

Of a compliment only a third is meant. *Welsh proverb*

' **1 Recognition of Ignorance**

To be conscious that you are ignorant is a great step to knowledge.
Benjamin Disraeli

2 Relatives

You recognize your relatives when they are rich.   *Yiddish proverb*

3 The Cure

The remedy is worse than the disease.

4 Repentance

It is never too late to repent.

5 Innocence

Repentance is good, but innocence better.

6 Injury

Revenge is a confession of pain.   *Latin proverb*

7 To Get Even

If you want to be revenged, hold your tongue.   *Spanish proverb*

8 Riches

Riches serve wise men, but command a fool.   *French proverb*

9 Slavery

A great fortune is a great slavery.   *Latin proverb*

10 Not Infallible

No one is always right.   **'**

' ## 1 Tardy

Who rises late must trot all day.

2 Error

What is the use of running, when you're on the wrong road?

3 Wear Out

Better to wear out than to rust out.

4 Be Ready

Prepare in youth for your old age.　　*Yiddish proverb*

5 Ego

Self-love never dies.　　*Voltaire*

6 When to Be Silent

He is not a fool who knows when to hold his tongue.

7 Real Eloquence

Silence is more eloquent than words.

8 Sympathize

Rejoice not in another's sorrow.　　*Turkish proverb*

9 The Right Sequence

First think, and then speak.

'

1 Who's Guilty

Whoever profits by the crime is guilty of it.   *French proverb*

2 Individualist

Who so would be a man must be a non-conformist.

Ralph Waldo Emerson

3 Confession

Confession is the first step to confession.   *English proverb*

4 How Brief

Life is but a day at most.   *Robert Burns*

' **Chinese Proverbs**

1 Brothers

If brothers disagree, the bystander takes advantage.

2 Waiting

To one who waits, a moment seems a year.

3 Endings

There are no feasts in the world which do not break up at last.

4 Wise Shopping

When you go out to buy, don't show your silver.

5 The Necessity of God

Without the aid of the divine, man cannot walk even an inch.

6 Usefulness of Man

If Heaven creates a man, there must be some use for him.

7 Ignorance

The more stupid, the happier.

8 Usefulness of Books

To open a book brings profit.

9 Education

Even if we study to old age we shall not finish learning. '

' 1 To Stop Drinking

If you want a plan by which to stop drinking, look at a drunken man when you are sober.

2 Barking Dogs

One dog barks at something, and a hundred bark at the sound.

3 Greatness

The great tree attracts the wind.

4 Insignificance of Man

Man's life is like a candle in the wind.

5 Inevitability of Death

For each man to whom Heaven gives birth, the earth provides a grave.

6 A Suitable Grave

Any place in the earth will do to bury a man.

7 The Way to Success

If you wish to succeed, consult three old people.

8 Inevitability of Age

Don't laugh at him who is old; the same will assuredly happen to us.

9 Good Example

By following the good you learn to be good.

10 All Have Failings

Among men, who is faultless? '

1 To Know a Man

If you wish to know the mind of a man, listen to his words.

2 Kindness

A single kind word keeps one warm for three winters.

3 The Tongue Is Dangerous

The tongue is like a sharp knife: it kills without drawing blood.

4 Duplicity

His mouth is honey, his heart a sword.

5 Fortune

A great fortune depends on luck, a small one on diligence.

6 Fame and Friendship

A well-known friend is a treasure.

7 Without Effort

Come easy, go easy.

8 Error

Men all make mistakes; horses all stumble.

9 Sleep

Sleep is a priceless treasure; the more one has of it the better it is.

10 Independence

A wise man makes his own decisions; an ignorant man follows public opinion.

(1 Economy

Economy makes men independent.

2 Goodness

You cannot make a good omelette out of rotten eggs.

3 Favours

Have no recollection of favours given; do not forget benefits conferred.

4 Gambling

If you believe in gambling, in the end you will sell your own house.

5 Value of the Aged

If a family has an old person in it, it possesses a jewel.

6 Peace and Order

If there is righteousness in the heart, there will be beauty in character. If there is beauty in character, there will be harmony in the home. If there is harmony in the home, there will be order in the nation. If there is order in the nation, there will be peace in the world.

7 Look for Value

Don't buy everything that's cheap.

8 The Price of Conquest

To joy in conquest is to joy in the loss of human life. **)**

8

Wit and wisdom through the ages

1 He's simply got the instinct for being unhappy highly developed.
Saki (Hector Hugh Munro)

2 I'm living so far beyond my income that we may almost be said to be living apart. *Saki*

3 No more privacy than a goldfish. *Saki*

4 I have never thought much of the courage of a lion-tamer; inside the cage he is, at least safe from other men. *George Bernard Shaw*

5 Inconsistency is the only thing in which men are consistent.
Horace Smith

6 Some folks are wise and some are otherwise. *Tobias Smollett*

7 There is a demand nowadays for men who can make wrong appear right. *Alfred Lord Tennyson*

8 In statesmanship, get the formalities right; never mind about the moralities. *Mark Twain*

6 **1** It is the proud perpetual boast of the Englishman that he never brags. *Wyndham Lewis*

2 We have two ears and one mouth that we may listen the more and talk the less. *Zeno*

3 Youth had been a habit of hers for so long that she could not part with it. *Rudyard Kipling*

4 Dunking is bad taste but tastes good. *Franklin Pierce Adams*

5 You never know what you can do without until you try.
Franklin Pierce Adams

6 Practical politics consists in ignoring facts. *Franklin Pierce Adams*

7 To force myself to earn more money, I determined to spend more.
James Agate

8 She used to diet on any kind of food she could lay her hands on.
Arthur 'Bugs' Baer

9 You can take a boy out of the country but you can't take the country out of a boy. *Arthur 'Bugs' Baer*

10 When I see a man of shallow understanding extravagantly clothed, I always feel sorry – for the clothes.
Josh Billings (Henry Wheeler Shaw)

11 We make more enemies by what we say than friends by what we do.
John Churton Collins **9**

1 Nothing deflates so fast as a punctured reputation.
Thomas Robert Dewar

2 It is much easier to be critical than correct. *Benjamin Disraeli*

3 What's fame after all? 'Tis apt to be what someone writes on your tombstone. *Finley Peter Dunne*

4 We are always getting ready to live, but never living.
Ralph Waldo Emerson

5 He is so mean, he won't let his little baby have more than one measle at a time. *Eugene Field*

6 The more you say, the less people remember. *François Fenelon*

7 How easy it is for a man to die rich, if he will but be contented to live miserable. *Henry Fielding*

' **1** Isn't your life extremely flat.
With nothing whatever to grumble at? *W. S. Gilbert*

2 Man is nature's sole mistake. *W. S. Gilbert*

3 No one can have a higher opinion of him than I have – and I think he is a dirty little beast. *W. S. Gilbert*

4 Genius is the talent of a man who is dead. *Edmond de Goncourt*

5 Discussing the characters and foibles of common friends is a great sweetener and cementer of friendship. *William Hazlitt*

6 The worst use that can be made of success is to boast of it.
Arthur Helps

7 A highbrow is the kind of person who looks at a sausage and thinks of Picasso. *Alan Patrick Herbert*

8 A hair in the head is worth two in the brush. *Oliver Herford*

9 Perhaps it was because Nero played the fiddle that they burned Rome. *Oliver Herford*

10 The brighter you are, the more you have to learn. *Don Herold*

11 If there's anything a public servant hates to do it's something for the public. *Frank McKinney Hubbard*

12 So far I haven't heard of anybody who wants to stop living on account of the cost. *Frank McKinney Hubbard*

13 The proper time to influence the character of a child is about a hundred years before he is born. **'**

1 The greatest animal in creation is the animal who cooks.
Douglas Jerrold

2 A man seldom thinks with more earnestness of anything than he does his dinner.   *Samuel Johnson*

3 My idea of an agreeable person is one who agrees with me.
Samuel Johnson

4 Whoever thinks of going to bed before twelve o'clock is a scoundrel.
Samuel Johnson

5 Of all noises, I think music is the least disagreeable.
Samuel Johnson

6 It is a great misfortune neither to have enough wit to talk well nor enough judgment to be silent.   *Jean de La Bruyère*

7 There are only two ways of getting on in the world: by one's own industry, or by the stupidity of others.   *Jean de La Bruyère*

8 We are never made as ridiculous through the qualities we have as through those we pretend to.   *François de la Rochefoucauld*

9 Men are able to trust one another, knowing the exact degree of dishonesty they are entitled to expect.   *Stephen Leacock*

10 The minute a man is convinced that he is interesting, he isn't.
Stephen Leacock

11 My first wife divorced me on grounds of incompatibility, and besides, I think she hated me.   *Oscar Levant*

12 God must have loved the plain people; he made so many of them.
Abraham Lincoln

'

1 Anger is never without a reason, but seldom a good one.
Benjamin Franklin

2 If you would know the value of money, go and try to borrow some.
Benjamin Franklin

3 If you would lose a troublesome visitor, lend him money.
Benjamin Franklin

4 Time and tide wait for no man, but time always stands still for a woman of thirty.   *Robert Frost*

5 As soon as you cannot keep anything from a woman, you love her.
Paul Geraldy

'

'

1 Hope is all right and so is Faith, but what I would like to see is a little Charity.   *Don Marquis*

2 In the main, there are two sorts of books: those that no one reads and those that no one ought to read.   *H. L. Mencken*

3 Many a live wire would be a dead one except for his connections.
Wilson Mizner

4 That must be wonderful; I don't understand it at all.   *Molière*

5 What orators lack in depth they make up for in length.
Baron de Montesquieu

6 There is nothing so consoling as to find that one's neighbour's troubles are at least as great as one's own.   *George Moore*

7 Practical prayer is harder on the soles of your shoes than on the knees of your trousers.   *Austin O'Malley*

8 Please return this book; I find that though many of my friends are poor arithmeticians, they are nearly all good bookkeepers.
Sir Walter Scott

9 What really flatters a man is that you think him worth flattering.
George Bernard Shaw

10 There are few wild beasts more to be dreaded than a talking man having nothing to say.   *Jonathan Swift*

11 Where all think alike, no one thinks very much.   *Walter Lippmann*

12 If you can't convince them, confuse them.   *Harry S Truman*   '

1 Home is where the college student home for the holidays isn't.
Laurence J. Peter

2 The most popular labour-saving device today is still a husband with money.   *Joey Adams*

3 If it were not for the intellectual snobs who pay, the arts would perish with their starving practitioners – let us thank heaven for hypocrisy.   *Aldous Huxley*

4 Man is ready to die for an idea, provided that idea is not quite clear to him.   *Paul Eldridge*

5 Knowledge is power, if you know it about the right person.
Ethel Watts Mumford

6 Logic – an instrument used for bolstering a prejudice.
Elbert Hubbard

7 All the historical books which contain no lies are extremely tedious.
Anatole France

8 Failure has gone to his head.   *Wilson Mizner*

9 We are tomorrow's past.   *Mary Webb*

10 I never think of the future. It comes soon enough.   *Albert Einstein*

11 Those who cannot remember the past are condemned to repeat it.
George Santayana

12 My guess is that well over 80 per cent of the human race goes through life without having a single original thought.
H. L. Mencken

1 Always willing to lend a helping hand to the one above him.
F. Scott Fitzgerald, of Hemingway

2 My belief is that to have no wants is divine.   *Socrates*

3 I never dared be radical when young
For fear it would make me conservative when old.   *Robert Frost*

4 The nation had the lion's heart. I had the luck to give the roar.
Winston Churchill

5 Some are bent with toil, and some get crooked trying to avoid it.

6 The advantage of a classical education is that it enables you to despise the wealth which it prevents you from achieving.
Russell Green

7 Education is a method by which one acquires a higher grade of prejudices.   *Laurence J. Peter*

8 Take away love and our earth is a tomb.   *Robert Browning*

9 A lie can travel halfway around the world while the truth is putting on its shoes.   *Mark Twain*

10 Man – a reasoning rather than a reasonable animal.
Alexander Hamilton

11 George Washington, as a boy, was ignorant of the commonest accomplishments of youth. He could not even lie.   *Mark Twain*

12 It is always the best policy to speak the truth, unless, of course, you are an exceptionally good liar.   *Jerome K. Jerome*

INDEX

References are given thus: '83(**7**)', which means 'page 83, entry **7**'.

babies 70(**5**), 74(**3**), 76(**1**), 85(**1**), 119(**1**),
129(**4**), 233(**5**)
bachelors 85(**2**)
Bacon, Francis 215(**1**)
bad jokes 34(**2**), 35(**3**), 159(**1**)
Baer, Arthur 'Bugs' 232(**8**), (**9**)
balding 11(**1**), (**2**), 85(**4**), 127(**6**)
Balfour, Arthur James 183(**1**)
bankruptcy 48(**4**)
banks 3(**1**), 14(**4**), 18(**5**), 39(**1**),69(**4**), 70(**3**),
101(**9**), 157(**3**); piggy 26(**2**)
bargains 85(**6**)
Barrie, James 123(**9**), 211(**3**)
barristers 38(**3**)
Barrymore, John 32(**1**)
Beaumarchais, Pierre Augustin de
195(**5**)
beauty 120(**1**), 197(**4**), 202(**3**), 230(**6**);
salons 6
Beecher, Henry Ward 186(**5**), 191(**1**)
Beethoven, Ludwig van 167(**4**)
beggars 12(**1**), 16(**2**), 218(**3**)
belief 199(**5**), 206(**5**)
Bell, Alexander Graham 168(**2**), 180(**1**)
benefactors 85(**7**), (**8**)
benevolence 85(**9**)
Bersohn, Robert 68(**1**)
bestsellers 86(**1**)
betting 98(**6**), 159(**8**); *see also* gambling
Bible 10(**1**), (**2**), 191(**2**), 197(**8**), 199(**1**),
211(**4**)
bicycles *see* cycling
Bierce, Ambrose 90(**9**), 92(**10**)
bigamy 85(**2**)
Billings, Josh *see* Shaw, Henry Wheeler
Bill of Rights for Boys (*Hoover*) 181(**1**)
bills 18(**3**), 42(**5**), 43(**6**), 76(**2**), 148(**8**),
154(**9**)
biographies 118(**7**)
biology 7(**5**), 34(**4**)
birth and reproduction 6(**6**), 14(**1**), 61(**1**),
86(**3**), 133(**1**), 228(**5**)
birthdays 16(**4**), 58(**6**), 66(**1**), 86(**4**), 164(**1**)
boasting 232(**1**), 234(**6**)
Bonaparte, Napoleon 3(**4**), 173(**4**), 174(**1**),
184(**3**), 190(**3**)
Book of Common Prayer 207(**2**), 218(**2**)
books 10(**1**), 89(**2**), 123(**8**), 131(**5**), 133(**3**),
197(**1**), 227(**8**), 237(**2**), (**8**), 238(**7**),
240(**6**); bestselling 86(**1**); classic 89(**4**);
new 122(**3**); rare 106(**4**); *see also* reading
boredom 122(**9**)

bores 28(**5**), 184(**5**)
Borge, Victor 182(**4**)
bosses *see* employers
boys 181(**1**)
Braun, Wernher von 179(**4**)
brevity 212(**7**); of life 226(**4**)
Bright, John 184(**4**)
British Rail 63(**2**)
brothers 227(**1**)
Browning, Robert 239(**8**)
Bruyère, Jean de La 235(**6**), (**7**)
budgets 86(**5**), (**6**), (**7**), (**8**), 132(**5**)
bureaucrats 154(**1**)
Burgess, Gellet 55(**1**)
Burnham, Daniel Hudson 178(**7**)
Burns, George 174(**5**)
Burns, Robert 221(**6**), 226(**4**)
bus: conductors 87(**1**); drivers 162(**5**);
school − 26(**3**)
business 49(**6**), 87(**23**), (**3**), (**4**), (**5**), (**6**),
90(**4**), 94(**5**), (**6**), 120(**3**), 141(**4**), 177(**2**),
178(**1**); economy 87(**3**); forecaster 87(**4**),
162(**6**); -man 87(**5**), (**6**); *see also*
executives; work(ers)
butterflies, flying speed of 170(**1**)
Buxton, Charles 187(**1**)

campaigning, political 175(**8**)
Canada 163(**1**), 170(**1**)
candidates 88(**1**), 175(**8**); *see also*
politicians
Canterbury, Archbishop of 131(**7**)
capital punishment 76(**4**)
Capp, Al 80(**2**)
Carlyle, Thomas 222(**1**)
Carnegie, Dale 180(**2**), 198(**1**)
cars, 17(**2**), 47(**2**), (**3**), 56(**1**), 57(**1**), 58(**1**),
(**5**), 82(**2**), 88(**2**), 93(**5**), 98(**1**), 99(**7**),
101(**6**), 111(**7**), 117(**1**), (**3**), 119(**3**), (**5**),
130(**4**), 138(**3**), 147(**7**), (**9**), 154(**4**), (**5**),
165(**3**); accidents 39(**7**), 117(**1**), (**3**),
119(**5**), 154(**5**); parking 116(**8**); second-
hand 20(**2**)
cats 35(**4**), 43(**5**), 94(**8**), 164(**1**); and mice
75(**3**)
caution 221(**4**)
cemeteries 18(**2**), 166(**2**)
centenarians 25(**4**), 88(**4**), 178(**2**)
Cervantes, Miguel de 167(**2**)
chairperson 88(**5**), (**6**)
change 115(**3**), (**6**), (**8**), 127(**4**), 157(**3**),
202(**5**)

Other Titles from Piatkus Books

If you have enjoyed *It Gives Me Great Pleasure,* you may be interested in other books published by Piatkus for after-dinner speakers and communicators. Titles include:

Confident Speaking: How to communicate effectively using the Power Talk system Christian Godefroy and Stephanie Barrat
My Lords, Ladies and Gentlemen: The best and funniest after-dinner stories from the famous Phyllis Shindler
100 Best After-Dinner Stories Phyllis Shindler
100 Favourite After-Dinner Stories From the Famous Phyllis Shindler
Powerspeak: The complete guide to public speaking and communication Dorothy Leeds
Raise Your Glasses: The best and wittiest anecdotes and after-dinner stories from the famous Phyllis Shindler

For a free brochure with further information on our range of titles, please write to:

> Piatkus Books
> Freepost 7 (WD 4505)
> London, W1E 4EZ

PIATKUS